Dress Your Dream Bed

Vintage Linen Inspirations for Today's Elegant Bed

Rita Farro

Published by

700 East State Street • Iola, WI 54990-0001
715/445-2214 • FAX: 715/445-4087   www.krause.com

Please call or write for our free catalog of publications. Our toll-free number to place an order or obtain a free catalog is 800-258-0929 or please use our regular business telephone 715-445-2214 for editorial comment and further information.

Library of Congress Catalog Number: 2001097833
ISBN: 0-87349-386-9

Acknowledgments

Bob Boyd of Boyd-Fitzgerald in Bettendorf, Iowa, did an incredible job on the photography for this book. Bob is quiet, patient and completely persnickety-all qualities I lack, but exactly what was needed to take fabulous pictures of beds. Brian Herrick of Lebeda Mattresses was the guy who came through with the actual beds. I don't know what we would have done without him. I'd also like to thank Kris Manty, my project manager at Krause Publications. She was professional at every turn, and always understood my passion for this subject

Judy Wilkinson of New York City is the best editor in the world. Judy made this a better book. She took out the flat parts, and had the good sense to tell me when I was going over the top. Believe it or not, I am sometimes capable of cliché and Judy saved you.

I need to thank Donna Babylon, Pamela Burke, Sue Hausmann, Debra Justice, Mary Mulari, Joanne Ross, Maureen Van Loon, and Nancy Zieman. They all contributed to this book. Donna Babylon came up with the perfect subtitle. Sue sent a huge box full of beautiful embroidered linens. The Viking Sewing Machine Company provided me with a Designer #1 to sew samples. Joanne Ross did a fabulous job of editing the chapter on laundering, and Pam Burke edited the chapter on embellishment. The quality of this book is greatly elevated because of the expertise of these women, and I appreciate their generosity.

The people pictured in the beds are my real family. I'd like to thank them for getting up at 5 a.m. to catch the morning light: My niece, Amy Bowe, and her son Cale (we call this photo "the blonde, the babe, and the back in the bed"); my niece, Kelcy Schroder; my nephew, Parker Kearney; and my might-as-well-be-a-niece, newlywed Carrie Fitzgerald Parrot. Our sweetest little model was Baby Lauren, only three weeks old at the time.

There never would have been a book if it wasn't for my home team-the sisters and cousins I grew up with, who still share my daily life. Debbie, Deena, Jackie, Kim, Linda, and Ronda. We go through it together, trying to figure it out. Marriage, children, birth, death, happy, sad. We give it our best. We cry, we laugh. We hold each other up. For this book, we did sewing projects at Ronda's, early photo sessions at Kim's-and spent long hours in the studio. I can't thank them enough. Especially my artistic cousin Linda, who was the most agreeable, enthusiastic, unpaid worker of all time. Because of what we learned while working on this book, we are all sleeping on better beds!

I can't forget the special teams. My friend Janet knew about Charisma™ sheets long before I did, and this book has become one more thing for us to share. My friend Bert was always there for me, if it was going to auctions, moving beds, or doing yet another photo shoot. And then, Val got called up to do the final proofreading of the book galleys-the job she was born to do. And, a special thanks to my Ya Ya sister, Mary Mulari. This book was born during a seminar we worked on together, and she is a part of almost every chapter.

New studies show that women who have good women friends live longer. If that's true, I'm gonna outlive my fabulous cotton sheets…

Contents

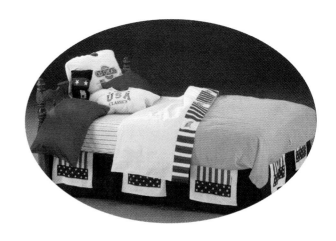

Introduction

The bed is the heart and soul of a home. My bed is made up with vintage linen—tatted edges, embroidered pillowcases, and an exquisite, soft wool-batt comforter. My son, Elliott, has a red, white, and blue quilt on his bed that I made from the mementos of his life. The little red satin embroidered baseball jacket he wore on his first day of kindergarten is in that quilt. When some kids go away to college, their mothers send boxes of homemade cookies; my son, Ross, got a package with a pillowcase that hung out on the line to dry. Surely, when he put it on his pillow, he'd go to sleep, smelling home, and feeling loved and connected.

For many years, I've been an avid collector of vintage bed linens, especially sheets and pillowcases, but I never wanted to just store them in my cedar chest. They should be used. That's the purpose of an every-day-ordinary-see-it-feel-it-and-smell-it wonder of a beautiful cotton sheet.

My first vintage sheet set came from an estate auction in DeWitt, Iowa, when I bid $1 for a box full of flat, white cotton sheets. Upon closer inspection, I discovered an embellished sheet with "OURS" embroidered in bright gold thread on the hem and a matching set of pillowcases with "MR." and "MRS." The set looked unused, as though it had been folded and stored—for decades.

We never had sheets like this when I was growing up and there certainly was nothing available like this in the stores where I shopped. I was excited about using this luxurious set. But, the "OURS" sheet was too short for our queen-size bed, so with great trepidation, I added a sheet "extender" and voila! I had officially modified my first vintage sheet.

As my confidence grew, I altered other sheets found at auctions or flea markets. Vintage sheets with extenders became my unique gift. I loved the old cotton so much, I made new pillowcases out of the flat double sheets and, eventually, I even figured out how to make a new fitted sheet from an old flat sheet.

Baby Lauren surrounded by vintage linen.

7

Well, you get the idea. Use these linens for the purpose for which they were intended. Put them on your bed. Feel them and smell them. Enjoy them. Keeping them hidden away in a trunk is like owning a Porsche, but driving a Yugo to work because you don't want to put miles on your beautiful sports car. It's like putting plastic slipcovers over your new furniture. Who are you protecting it from? Your family? If you pack something away for 50 years, it won't have any special meaning for your children because they won't ever have seen it. So, after you die, it goes to the Goodwill store and some stranger will be very grateful for the pristine condition you kept it in.

Aunt Rozella was one of the most important people in my life. My family ate Thanksgiving dinner at her house every November for 35 years. After she died, Uncle Marion moved into town, and I was helping him pack up his things for an auction. I was stunned to find a set of sterling silverware hidden under her bed. Her pattern, Spring Glory, had been collected one piece at a time over 17 years. All the original receipts were still in the beautiful wooden box along with the silverware. Uncle Marion said she never used it, not even once. I sat on the edge of her bed, missing her, wondering what special occasion she had been saving Spring Glory for. At the auction several weeks later, I bought Aunt Rozella's silver. My family cheered for me that day, and we use it often—for the purpose for which it was intended.

That's the whole point of this book. I believe we should use our very best stuff every single day. I don't keep Spring Glory under my bed. It sits out on my kitchen counter. When the four of us eat a meal together—whether it's Christmas dinner or tacos on a Sunday afternoon—we use Aunt Rozella's sterling and white linen napkins. Life itself is the special occasion. The whole point is to show your family, in any way you can, how much you love them. Maybe the best way is through the everyday stuff: the meals you eat, the conversations you have, and the time you spend together.

In this house, for my family, the love is also in the beds they sleep on.

Chapter 1

The Naked Truth About Cotton

Y ou should sleep naked. The feel of cotton on bare skin is as comforting as the sound of a purring kitten and as delicious as the taste of a Godiva chocolate truffle. Cool, soft cotton touching my skin renews my spirit and refreshes my soul. If you're not naked, what's the point of even having fabulous bedding?

Original paper label for Pequot sheets.

Well, okay, wear that nightgown, but I want you to know what you're missing.

My obsession with cotton sheets coincided with my raging hot flashes. Cotton absorbs moisture, wicking away excess body heat. I thought buying new "100 percent cotton" sheets was the answer, but some sheets were definitely better than others.

There is more to this cotton thing than just fabric content. For example, there's thread count. Thread count (or TC) is how manufacturers describe their fabric. The higher the number, the finer the thread. In the 1970s, we bought muslin sheets with a 144 TC. But, like Farrah Fawcett's hairdo, that's a thing of the past (nobody misses the hairdo *or* the sandpaper sheets). A thread count of 180 or more is considered percale. Today's standard for luxury sheets is more like 220. My husband John tells people our sheets have a thread count of 3,000 (not true).

My growing passion for 100 percent cotton bedding was nurtured by my lifelong love of auctions. One day, I bought an old white flat sheet with a "Pequot" label on it. This was an extraordinary sheet, and even though I had no idea what the TC was, it was clearly better than any of my new stuff I'd purchased. It was heavy and crisp, with a wonderful smooth finish.

I put an extender on the end, and this Pequot beauty became my favorite sheet to sleep under. But I didn't know why it felt so superior—until I stumbled across a little book called *The Story of Pequot*.

This type of wonderful coincidence is a well-known phenomenon. My friends call it "Ritaluck," and it is especially handy when I'm looking for parking spaces at the mall or trying to buy tickets for sold-out Elton John concerts.

This fascinating 31-page booklet, written for the Naumkeag Steam Cotton Company in 1929, explains how they used to pick cotton in the fields down South, bale it, and deliver it to the big textile mills in New England.

My treasured little booklet describes the importance of long staple "fibres" (that was the spelling they used). Every bale was carefully checked before the cotton could be accepted. "No cotton is considered fit for Pequot sheets and pillow cases unless it [the cotton fiber] is at least one and 1/16 inches long."

According to the booklet, "The Pequot label lends as much distinction to sheeting as the hall mark does to silver." No wonder I loved my Pequot sheet. In 1929, Naumkeag Mills was turning out 25,000 miles of sheeting a year. Enough to "girdle the earth at its equator, with a few miles to spare for hem."

The mystery of my exceptional Pequot sheet was beginning to make sense.

In my continuing efforts to discover why my vintage treasures seemed so superior to newer cottons, my research led me to Pamela Alspaugh of the International Textile Center in Lubbock, Texas. I could have listened to her talk all day. That southern drawl just hypnotizes me.

According to Ms. Alspaugh, "The very best sheets are made out of ELS—Extra Long Staple—which is a variety of cotton. The three ELS cottons grown in the world are PIMA, Egyptian, and Sea Island."

I asked, "Why is there so much Egyptian Cotton on the market? In the malls, at discount stores—it's everywhere. Do they grow that much cotton in Egypt?"

Ms. Alspaugh laughed and said, "No, honey, Egypt is itty bitty when it comes to total cotton production. Why, if Texas was a country, we'd rank No. 5 on the world market for cotton production. Egypt is way down the list."

Ms. Alspaugh said the most knowledgeable person in the world about cotton bedding was Frank Garnier, retired vice president and director of cotton purchasing for Fieldcrest/Cannon.

I loved listening to Mr. Garnier talk about his 40 years in the cotton industry. He told me how, many years ago, Firestone cultivated PIMA cotton to provide the cording in its tires. Then, "After World War II, nylon was developed." He was an absolute treasure trove of information. He told me about a lawsuit awhile back—The American PIMA Growers went to court because a towel manufacturer put "PIMA" on the labels of towels that were only 5 percent PIMA.

Bingo. That "Egyptian" thing was beginning to make sense. Manufacturers can mix a very small percentage of Egyptian yarn with inferior grades of cotton and still label it "Egyptian." Bummer.

According to Mr. Garnier, "In many ways, the best cotton in the world is grown right here in America. SUPIMA™ is a registered trademark of the American PIMA Growers Association."

If a sheet has SUPIMA on the label, that means it is made

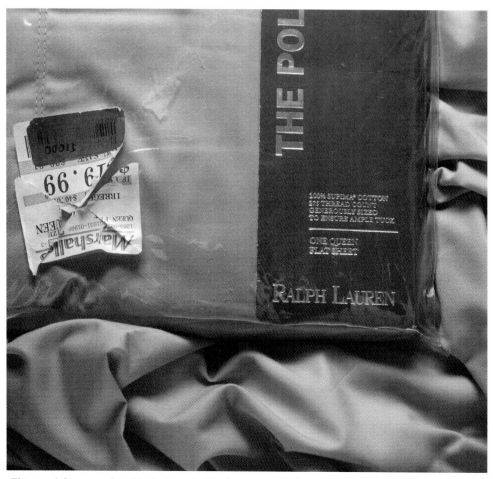

This set of sheets was found in the bargain bin. Can you read "Supima?"

from 100 percent PIMA (extra-long staple) cotton fibers. When it says SUPIMA, you can be sure about what you're getting." Wow. I didn't know that. This could be the most exciting thing I learn this year.

After talking to Ms. Alspaugh and Mr. Garnier, I understood what was so extraordinary about my vintage Pequot sheets—and I also knew what I was looking for in a new sheet. SUPIMA. That's the ticket.

According to Mr. Garnier, Fieldcrest developed a 310-count SUPIMA luxury cotton sheet to compete with the Italian imports. This extraordinary sheet is called Charisma. They sell at the finest department stores for about $400 a set. I called all the stores near my home, but nobody carried Charisma sheets. I remembered that my friend Janet will only sleep on Charisma sheets. She's been praising them for years, but I had no idea what she was talking about. I have never owned a set of these fabulous sheets myself.

I wrote this book primarily as a mission to bring vintage linens out of the cedar chest and put them back onto the bed. But I realize not everybody has a stash of heirloom bedding, so the question is, how do you shop for new bed linens that will rival the feel and the look of those great old heirloom treasures?
Look for three things:

- 🖾 The fabric content (100 percent cotton)
- 🖾 The thread count (above 180 for percale)
- 🖾 The "hand"

Mr. Garnier says the "hand" is really the most important, yet the most difficult, to explain. You will find many 100 percent cotton sheets on the market with impressively high thread counts. But they may be woven out of inferior, shorter staple cotton. That can only be determined by feeling and touching the cotton, unless you see the word SUPIMA. Remember—that word is a registered trademark for the American PIMA Growers Association and means that sheet is 100 percent PIMA cotton.

As my love and understanding of cotton bed linens grew, I searched for embellished sheets and pillowcases at every auction and estate sale. I felt like a '49er digging for gold. I bought beautiful bed linens that had been stored in cedar chests and closets for years. That "Ritaluck," y'know?

This genuine full-blown obsession with vintage cotton bed linens soon filled up every spare inch of my house. I had no choice but to write a book about it.

We spend one-third of our lives in bed. Your bed should be that soft place to fall into at the end of your day. A haven. Why not make it the one place in the world where you feel pampered and special?

An elegant bed is an everyday, affordable luxury. It's not like buying a Mercedes or taking a trip to Paris. Many of the things photographed for this book were purchased at auctions, estate sales, and flea markets.

Whether you are shopping for new linens to embellish and trim or revamping vintage heirlooms to fit your queen size bed, dressing a beautiful bed is a powerful way to show your family how much you love them. Do it for the people you love.

Better yet—do it for yourself!

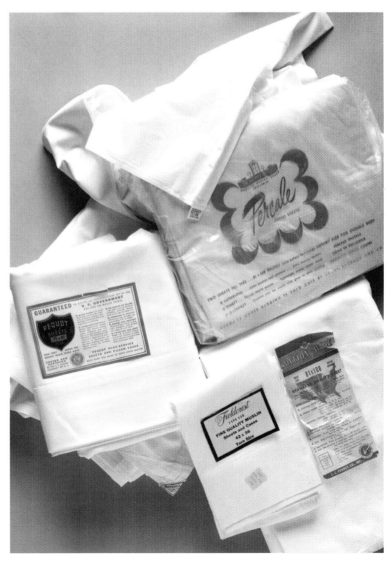

"Nationwide" was the JC Penney's store brand, "Fieldcrest" was Marshall Field's, and "Harmony House" was Sear's.

Chapter 2

It All Comes Out In The Wash

*I*n a perfect world, all vintage bed linen would have
been wrapped in acid-free paper, then lovingly stored
in a climate-controlled, cedar-lined closet. Dream on.

Old sheets, quilts, and pillowcases have often been stored improperly, causing staining or even serious damage. Remember, they didn't have Martha Stewart back then. If there is damage to the fabric, the piece may be unsalvageable. These two baby pillowcases, pictured at right, were starched, then stored for 50 years. They look beyond help, eh? But vintage cotton is very hearty, and even the worst discoloration can often be removed with a little persistence and a gentle hand.

A BIG disclaimer applies here. I am not a textile curator working in a museum. If you have a piece that is so valuable you couldn't bear to damage it, you should not risk washing it or using it on your bed. Wrap it up and take it out to admire every once in awhile. This book is about getting vintage linens back on the bed.

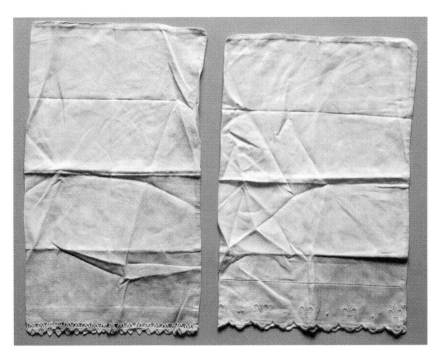

With the right care, even vintage linen that looks beyond help can be brought back to life.

When I write about "vintage linens," I am using the word as a generic term to mean sheets, pillowcases, etc. Not to be confused with actual "linen" fabric woven from flax. However, my personal "linen collection" is made up almost entirely of cotton things. If you're not sure what you have, take it to somebody who can identify the fabric before you proceed.

Joanne Ross is the chair of the Sewing and Stitchery Expo in Puyallup, Washington, and the Pierce County Cooperative Extension Office. She has a master's degree in clothing and textiles, and has an enormous collection of vintage linens. We try never to go to the same auctions. If you are uncertain about the fabric of your vintage piece, she suggests taking it to your county extension office. Those folks are very knowledgeable, and if they don't know, they will at least know whom to ask.

Joanne says these three things need to happen for cleaning to take place:

❎ Mechanical action (agitator or hand rubbing)

❎ Chemical action (soap or detergent)

❎ Thermo action (temperature of the water)

If you lower any of these from normal recommendations, you must increase one or both of the others to compensate. For example: cooler water, more detergent needed; less detergent, longer agitation. Get the idea? You can substitute the sun for agitation and strong chemicals—sun is thermo and chemical action. Longer soaking in place of agitation, thus using milder chemicals.

According to Joanne, most detergents are formulated for 70 degrees or above. So if the water is too cold, you will have poor results. Also, *hard* water redeposits minerals such as calcium or magnesium, making your laundry gray or dull-looking.

What's the difference between soap and detergent? Joanne was actually pleased to explain this to me. You can imagine she doesn't get asked these questions very often. Soap is made from animal fats and alkali (lye was used in olden days), while detergents are made from petroleum and natural fats and oils. You would not use detergents to take a bath nor would you use soaps to do your laundry on a regular basis. Think of it this way: when you take a bath with soap, you get scum around the tub. Eventually, the scum would ruin the working parts in your washing machine. Detergents have additives to alter the properties of the water and soil, allowing the water to penetrate the fibers; detergents also have builders which soften the water and maintain the necessary alkalinity.

Whew! That's what happens when you ask a REAL expert, folks…waaaay more than you wanted to know, eh? I am delighted to have Joanne's knowledgeable input for this important chapter. Proper laundering is the first step in getting those vintage linens out of the attic and back on your bed.

The Three-Step Revitalization

1. The Water Treatment

The first thing to do with a vintage piece of cotton or linen is to soak it in tepid water for several hours or overnight. If the item has been stored for many years, the thread has become extremely dry and is most fragile at this point. Natural fibers, cotton, and linen are revitalized by water—much like dehydrated mushrooms which must be soaked before you can cook with them.

Fabric becomes stronger when wet, so that's the first step: *Soak* your vintage linens—then you can begin to wash them in earnest. Dry fabric simply can't absorb or respond to soap or cleaner. Putting any pre-treatment on dry fabric is a waste of time and money.

2. GENTLE LAUNDERING

The second step, after soaking, is a gentle laundering. Most of the time, a regular washing machine on a delicate cycle is fine. Use a product meant for fragile fibers such as Ivory Soap™, or Orvis™. Be sure the cleaning product is completely dissolved before adding the item to be washed. Put the wet item into the tub of the machine, along with several old white terry cloth bath-towels to increase the agitation. Use warm water for the wash and cold water for the rinse. Do at least one extra cold-water rinse. Two is better. The point is to get out the leftover residue.

In either case, whether you're using a machine, or doing it by hand, always start with the most gentle laundry product and rinse completely. Several times.

3. DRY IN THE SUN

The third thing I do is hang the linens outside to dry in the sun. This is the best natural bleaching agent in the world. You just can't beat this affect on old cotton. For whitening, you get a double whammy if you can lay your wet linens on top of green grass to dry in the sun. Something about pho-tosynthesis…(I wish I'd paid more attention in seventh grade science class.) My friend Mary did this with a set of dingy damask napkins and she made me a believer.

Vintage linens should never be put into an electric or gas clothes dryer. Dryers are too hot and they shrink fabric, especially cotton. If you cannot hang things outside to dry, hang them on a rack in the house.

Joanne says, "The only thing a gas or elec-tric clothes dryer is good for is bath towels and your husband's underwear." I couldn't agree more.

To review: About 80 percent of the time, these three things will bring vintage linens back to life:

✑ First, soaking.
✑ Second, gentle washing.
✑ Third, drying in the sun.

Tip:
If an item is hand-sewn or has a lot of open work or lace, never put it in a washing machine. The open areas might get caught in the agitator and that would destroy the piece. Use a big sink or your bathtub instead. Joanne puts her delicate linens in a zippered pillowcase to protect them from the agitator. Mary prefers a mesh bag.

Go a Little Deeper

If, after the three-step revitalization process, you are still not happy with the look of your vintage cotton, there are several things to try. As you continue to work on the item, do not let the sheet and/or pillowcase dry in between treatments. Be persistent—experiment. You never can tell what's going to finally "do the trick" on a particular item. Do not get discouraged. Be patient.

"Pretreat" means to apply the cleaning solution to the *wet fabric*, and allow to stand for one hour. If the fabric dries before you get a chance to launder it again, wet it down, and wait another hour. Here is a list of my favorite cleaning products.

- Old fashioned bar of laundry soap, like Fels Napta™, or ZOTE™ soap. While the fabric is wet, rub the soap on the stain. Pretreat for one hour, put the item through another washing cycle, and see how it comes out.

- Fresh lemon juice. Depending on what caused the stain (and you really don't know), lemon juice has an enzyme that can be very effective. Again, apply the lemon juice to *wet* fabric, and allow it to sit for an hour.

- Shampoo can be exactly the right agent to break down yellow oily stains, especially if the stains are on a pillowcase, which means they're probably caused by hair oil. My cousin Jackie gave me this tip, and it works great. Apply the shampoo as a pre-treatment and wait the usual hour. (Use sparingly, as it will *really* suds up in your washing machine.) Joanne says pick a shampoo that has little or no dye and/or perfume.

- Hydrogen peroxide will remove some difficult mystery stains. If you have rust spots, try dipping the spot in a mixture of 1/2 cup hydrogen peroxide, 1/2 cup water, and 1/4 cup lemon juice. Dip and rinse…dip and rinse. This gently breaks down the stain. *Joanne's caution:* Do not use this on colors, silk, or wool.

- Vinegar is another one of those common sense, old-fashioned laundry boosters. Nothing removes musty odors better than white vinegar. My friend Bert inherited a wonderful old quilt top from her grandmother. Unfortunately, it had been stored in a musty basement—and the smell would knock your socks off from a distance of 50 feet.

Yikes! She soaked the quilt top in her bathtub overnight to let the cotton thread swell up and gain strength. The next day, she drained that water, and added some fresh warm water along with 2 cups of white vinegar. Sloshing it around in the tub, she repeated the process several times. Eventually, she washed her prized quilt top with Orvis (a mild soap recommended for washing quilts). The quilt top got fresh and clean. After hanging it outside, it even became fresh smelling. Again, there's *nothing* like hanging cotton outside to dry in the sunshine. Joanne says vinegar can be added to the rinse water to remove soap and detergent residue. One cup per load will do.

- Borax™ or Calgon™ are excellent additives, especially if you have hard water. They soften your water, which makes a tremendous difference in how the soap dissolves and works. You'll get a much better result. Do not confuse them with fabric softeners, which is a whole different breed of product. Fabric softeners can add a greasy residue that may cause discoloring.

- Baking soda can be very effective, depending on what kind of stain or discoloration you're dealing with. Make a paste of baking soda and water and use it as a pre-treatment.

- Ammonia is what Joanne recommends to remove musty and smoke smells. Use it half strength, soak for an hour, and rinse well. Then proceed.

- Oxi Clean™ is the new kid on the block when it comes to laundry products. It's extremely effective, yet very gentle. It's also kind of pricey—$20 for a two-pound box. Joanne loves this stuff. I can tell you that the bedding in her guest room is exquisite, and her vintage sheets are snowy white.

The Worst of the Worst

So, you did the standard three-step revitalization. Then, you tried the gentle remedies. But you're still not happy? There are more options. But, at some point, you may risk damaging the item.

Use common sense when dealing with vintage linens. When you think about it, most stains are only going to show if they're on the top 12 inches of the sheet or on the embellished side of a pillowcase. So, why punish the entire sheet or pillowcase to get out a spot that nobody is ever going to notice?

However, if your heirloom linen is not usable, you may decide to go even further, but **proceed with caution**. Here are some specific treatments for specific problems:

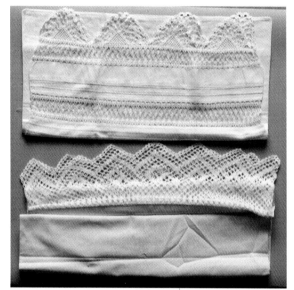

Before
Discolored by old starch.

After
An overnight soak in dishwasher detergent
finally did the trick.

DINGY OR GRAY

When linens have been stored for years, dingy gray will set in. In the old days, hard water made it impossible for the detergent to rinse out completely. That detergent residue or old starch will discolor the original white fabric. The two pillowcases above were yellowed after years of storage. They went through the three-step program, but were still dingy. I washed them several times in various detergents and tried Oxi-Clean. This is what finally did the trick:

> I soaked them in a solution of very hot water and a cup of dishwasher detergent. After an overnight soak in the machine, I ran a regular wash and rinse cycle. Then, I ran another cycle with Murphy's Oil Soap™ and rinsed them twice in cold water. Finally! White!

UNSIGHTLY SPOT OR STAIN

Here's a technique you might try to push a stain through the fibers of your vintage piece. Dip the stained area in a cleaning solution (from the list of my favorites on pages 18-19). Lay the item flat on top of a dry terry cloth towel. Then, using a soft toothbrush, gently brush at the wet spot, going in both directions. Add dry salt. The salt acts as an abrasive, to push the stain down into the dry towel. Repeat the process several times—wet, salt, and brush. This can be very effective on some stubborn stains.

DANGER ZONE

Every expert will tell you chlorine bleach is the big taboo when you're working with vintage linens. It's like trying to dry your hair with a blow torch. Although it will work, your hair might catch on fire. Chlorine could eat holes in your vintage cotton. Several bleach products on the market are non-chlorine. Try them first.

Having told you never to use chlorine bleach, here is how and why I sometimes do. Remember, I only resort to chlorine bleach if the stain is so disagreeable I can't use the pillowcase or sheet.

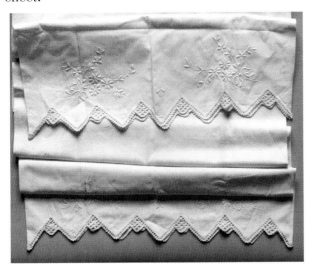

Before
Very stubborn brown stains.

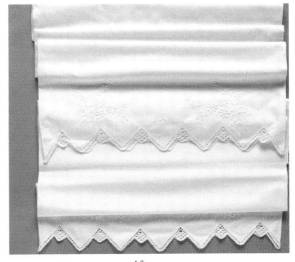

After
Results of Mary's whitening soak.

YELLOWING

Some pillowcases get especially yellowed and many women believe it's caused by their husband's "hair oil." This set looked impossible. I'd tried every trick in the book and after more launderings than I care to count, I decided they were unusable the way they were. So, even if it meant damage, I decided to try this concoction from Mary Mulari (my special Ya Ya Sister). She uses this now and then on her pillowcases to remove those nasty yellow stains. She calls it a "whitening soak":

> 🐝 Combine 1/2 cup of bleach and 1/4 cup of dishwasher detergent dissolved in a gallon of hot water. Soak your pillowcases for 30 minutes and then wash as usual.

Be observant. If your husband's pillowcases are the only ones that develop the yellow staining, make sure he never gets a vintage cotton, tatted pillowcase on his side of the bed. Buy him some Kmart Blue-Light specials and spare your good stuff.

Mary's whitening soak is also very effective in breaking down old starch stains. Of course, starch was very popular 50 years ago, and many of these vintage pieces were put into trunks or cedar chests after being beautifully starched and ironed. But that old starch can turn ugly brown and it's a tough stain to break down. As you can see from these before and after pictures, the little baby pillowcases finally did come back to a snowy white. The damage on the one little case was caused because the machine agitator caught the hem, and the hemstitching acted like a perforation. I could have prevented this damage if I'd put the case into a mesh bag.

Joanne recommends Oxi Clean as a whitening soak. She dissolves 2 tablespoons in 5 gallons of water in her washing machine and lets the stained items soak overnight. In the case of these little baby cases, I had to go all the way to chlorine bleach.

NOTHING-CUTS-IT-STAIN

Here, the stain I'm talking about is not only disagreeable, it's in a prominent place. You've tried everything previously mentioned. You've decided a mended hole would be preferable to the unsightly stain. Only then should you resort to this more determined variation of the chlorine bleach treatment:

> 🐝 Put 1/3 cup of chlorine bleach into a small bowl, with 2/3 cup of water. Do this procedure standing at a sink with running water. Pull the stained part of the item out so that it is the only part that gets dipped into the bleach solution. Dip it and wait for just a moment—then, immediately rinse the dipped spot under warm water and inspect the stain. If it is still there, continue to dip and rinse—always looking after each dip to see if the stain came out.

Using chlorine bleach is risky, but honestly, sometimes it's

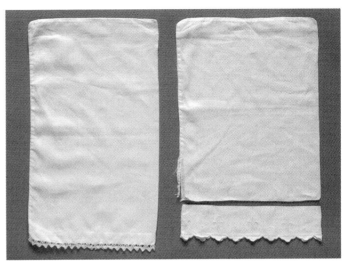

Before
This is what 50 years of poorly stored old starch looks like.

After
It took a dozen launderings, including Mary's chlorine soak, but I finally got them white. But the delicate hemstitching tore away because I didn't put it in a mesh bag. My own fault.

the only thing that works. I have had good success with this dip-and-rinse procedure, and it's been a couple of years since I caused a hole in anything. But it definitely could happen.

Don't get discouraged. You may try several different products before you obtain the results you want. Remember to work your way up—from the most gentle cleaning products and techniques to the more aggressive treatments.

The most important thing is to be patient. Serious discoloration or staining takes decades to develop. I once washed a set of pillowcases over and over for six days before they were white again. I lost track of the number of different treatments I tried. Joanne says to remember that time is your best friend. "If at first you don't succeed…well, try and try again."

You're doing the right thing by rescuing vintage linens from the attic, washing them, and bringing them back into daily use. Sheets and pillowcases are meant to be used—to be enjoyed. Remember Aunt Rozella's silver?

Chapter 3

Let It All Hang Out

When I take my sheets off the line, I hold them close to my face for just a moment and breathe them in. That fresh line-dried cotton smell makes me very happy and I can almost hear Tina Turner singing, "Simply The Best."

When I was a kid, Monday was laundry day. Mom would announce, proudly: "I had the lines full of sheets before 7:00"—like she'd just won a rodeo competition. She would be very catty about that neighbor woman who didn't get her sheets hung out until after lunch. Her tone implied that a family with such a lazy mother would never amount to much.

Even after my mother acquired the modern conveniences of an automatic washer and a fancy gas dryer, she always hung her sheets outside to dry. Winter or summer. If there was deep snow on the ground, Dad would shovel a path out to the clothesline. With women's liberation, we've come a long way, baby. My sisters and I all shovel our own paths.

My sisters, Ronda and Deena, and I have clothes poles in our respective yards made of two hedge trees with just the right "Y" joint, a unique housewarming gift from our father. We all hang our bedding outside to dry.

However, my sister, Debbie, lives in one of those new housing subdivisions with covenants against outside clotheslines. I worry about people who would legislate against hanging clothes outside. If they can't tolerate my sheets on a clothesline, they'd have to call 911 when they saw the 72 pink flamingos dancing on my porch.

My Mom had some pretty high standards when it came to hanging up her laundry. The underwear all marched along, color coded and size sorted. The socks were paired while still wet as she pulled them out of the basket. Unfortunately, those rules and skills are lost to my generation. I admit the only thing I hang outside is my bedding—and never before 7 a.m. I actually prefer my sheets to hang overnight for the evening dew, or, if I'm lucky, through a thunderstorm. Nothing smells better than a fresh rain rinse.

Clothesline Hardware

The placement of your lines is important. The biggest issue is the direction the wind blows at your house. Your clothes should flap in the breeze—not get blown down the length of the line. For example, at my house, the wind blows from west to east; so, my lines run from north to south. Your clothes should hang in full sun away from big trees (and bird do-do).

You can still buy metal clothes poles today at hardware stores. Get the heavy-duty sturdy ones. They sell for about $30 a pair. Dig two deep holes and mix up a bag of concrete to plant your poles in, 10 to 20 feet apart.

If that sounds like too much work, be creative. Look around.

My cousin Linda strung a line between two trees in her back yard. My friend Janet in California has a fenced-in back yard. She strung a clothesline from her back door to a fence post. Because of her strict neighborhood covenants, Jan rushes to get her laundry off the lines before the neighbors come home from work, although I'm sure they have more important things to worry about.

If you don't have a suitable place in your yard to string a long clothesline, you could make due with one of those little aluminum umbrella clotheslines. (I hope you're only renting.) My cousin Jackie put one of those up in her ritzy subdivision and they never did issue a warrant for her arrest.

Then, there are the lines themselves and the pins you use. I

Old-fashioned clothespin holders.

prefer the plastic-wrapped clothesline wire, and I like the modern snapping clothespins (probably invented the year I was born).

On the previous page is a picture of a "clothespin" caddy. It hangs on a hook near my basement door. If the pin caddy were left to hang on the line all the time, the fabric would soon rot. My Grandmother used to make them out of little baby dresses.

Hanging Procedures

First, take a wet rag with you to wipe down the clothesline. Then, fold your sheets from end to end. If there is an embellished edge, fold it down, so as not to encounter the direct sunlight. Hang the sheet by the open ends, with the embellished edge hanging over the line. Use one clothespin to hold the corners of two pillowcases together. I also like to fold down the embellished top edge of a pillowcase. Make sure everything is straight when you hang it. After the wind whips it, you won't even need to iron. I never iron my cotton sheets and pillowcases—that would ruin the wonderful fragrance of the line drying.

I also hang my quilts and blankets outside to dry. But you have to be very careful, because the weight of the water in a wool blanket or cotton quilt can cause two big problems. First of all, if you were to hang the blanket and/or quilt directly on the line, from the corners, the water would cause distortion and pull the blanket out of shape. All that weight could even damage the edges you were hanging it from. Also, such a heavy load could stretch your clothesline down to the ground. So, be sure to make a "cradle" out of an old sheet to spread the weight to two different clotheslines, preventing the stretching of your blanket. If you have a protected area (no animals), it might be safer to lay the quilt or blanket flat on the grass, on top of a white sheet.

Every so often, you'll need to re-tighten your lines, as the weight of wet laundry will eventually stretch them. My Mom had a long wooden pole with a notch in the end to prop her lines up in the middle. I don't do that either, Mom.

The smell of line-dried cotton always takes me back, if only for a heartbeat, to my own childhood—to long lazy summer days on the farm, helping Mom do the laundry, and folding crisp cotton sheets as they came, warm, off the line. Hanging my family's linens outside to dry is a gift I'm giving to them. It's the same gift my mother gave to her family. She would be very pleased to know I'm passing it on.

Mom would understand the connection I feel, through these old cotton linens, with her and her mother, and her mother's mother. And Tina Turner.

Tip:
I don't iron sheets. For one thing, I think it ruins the wonderful fragrance. Also, as my hero Erma Bombeck once said, "My second favorite household chore is ironing. My first being hitting my head on the top bunk bed until I faint."

Chapter 4

Making The Case

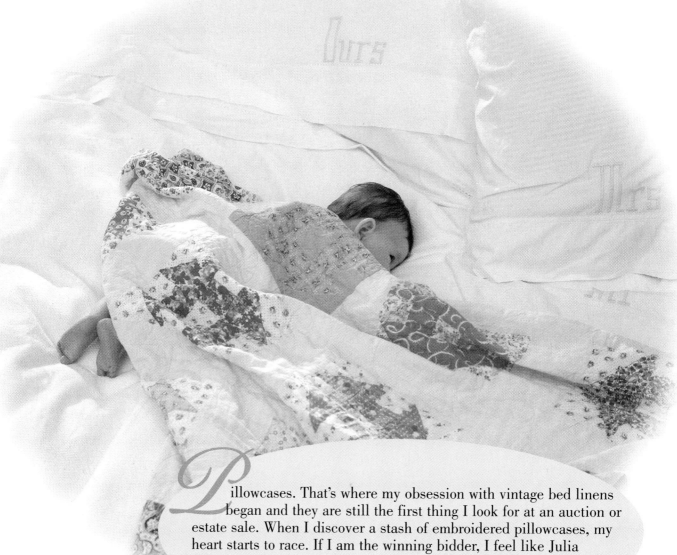

Pillowcases. That's where my obsession with vintage bed linens began and they are still the first thing I look for at an auction or estate sale. When I discover a stash of embroidered pillowcases, my heart starts to race. If I am the winning bidder, I feel like Julia Roberts accepting the Academy Award for "Erin Brockovich."

If the bed is the heart and soul of a home, the pillowcases are the heart and soul of the bed. You can tell a lot about a family just by looking at the pillowcases. To illustrate, let's go back 70 years or so and compare the pillowcases of two different families.

First, a family I know well, the Little family of Princeton, Iowa. My dad's family lived on a farm. His mother, Pearl Little, sewed pillowcases, shown at right, from unbleached muslin that came into her home as sacks containing chicken feed or flour. During the Depression, those muslin sacks were like gold to her. Besides pillowcases, Pearl also made dresses, curtains, quilts, and dishtowels. We all remember her famous wraparound aprons that had only cross-over straps—no ties.

My Aunt Glad, who was born in 1911, told me that, as a young housewife, she loved to go to the feed store with Uncle Barney to "pick out a new dress." Each sack was only one yard of fabric, so she had to make sure he bought two that were alike. Once the companies realized the farm wives were reusing the muslin in this way, they started printing the muslin sacks in bright calico patterns, blue stripes, small patterned yellow flowers with soft green leaves, etc. These prints were a marketing tool to sell chicken feed. Happily, today's fabric manufacturers have recreated many of those beautiful old calicos.

Pearl might simply add a 3-inch hem of contrasting calico fabric to her plain muslin pillow-

Top: Muslin flour sacks, trimmed with chicken feed calicos, circa 1930s.
Bottom: Pillowcases embroidered with crochet trim, circa 1950.

Fine linen and monograms from the Wrigley family.

Pillowcases from the Little family.

cases; or, she might embroider a colorful flower pattern to brighten them up. She liked to finish her pillowcases off with a crocheted edge around the opening.

In contrast, consider the pillowcases of the Wrigley family of Evanston, Illinois (of Wrigley Gum, and yes, Wrigley Field fame), shown above and on the next page. I am not related to this family, but I did get a glimpse of their pillowcases. They had stacks of little baby pillowcases made of very fine cotton batiste, trimmed with delicate handmade lace. No Wrigley baby ever laid his little face down on unbleached muslin.

The pillowcases for the grownups of the Wrigley family were made from a fine white cotton percale fabric with a very high thread count; or maybe a crisp white linen, considered the most luxurious fabric, even back then. There would be an elegant, deep hemstitch around the opening of the case. The edges might have a complicated scallop, or a wide border of hand-

Elegant bed linens—white thread on fine white fabric.

made lace. The Wrigley pillowcases were heirloom quality, made of pintucks and ladder stitches; intricate pulled-thread designs and/or open cutwork. The pillowcases, as well as the family sheets, would often be monogrammed. Monogramming was very popular with wealthy families. They also monogrammed their best tablecloths, napkins, and handkerchiefs. All of the intricate embroidery and thread work on the bed linen, including the monograms, was done with white thread.

We see two striking differences between the bed linens of the Little family and the Wrigleys. First, the fabric itself: muslin versus high-thread-count fine cotton. Second, the color of the embellishment itself. The Little linens were colorful—pink flowers with green leaves and blue birds. The Wrigley linens were white on white. Always. Snowy white thread on pristine white cotton or linen.

There isn't such an obvious class distinction today when it comes to bed linens. We've come a long way, baby. Actually, more like we've come full circle. For decades, bedding was always made out of 100 percent cotton or even linen. Then, in the 1950s, the manufacturers started to add polyester to make sheets and pillowcases "wrinkle-free," and by the time The Bee Gees were making it big, everything was a polyester/cotton blend. But a few years ago, 100 percent cotton sheets and pillowcases started making a come-back, showing up even at the discount stores. A TC of 180 is considered "percale," but today a 220 TC is not uncommon. All the major department stores (even Penney's, Sears, and Target) carry a nice line of cotton sheets.

My sisters and I went to Ireland last year, staying at bed and breakfasts. Although I don't remember this, Ronda swears that when my head hit the pillow on that first night, I said, in a very haughty tone, "Darn. Polyester." Even in Ireland, a country renowned for its fine linen, we were surrounded by 50/50 poly/cotton. Go figure.

Back here in the good old USA, high-thread-count, 100 percent cotton sheets and pillowcases are more available, but they are expensive. You can pay $50 to $200 for a set of pillowcases. But, take heart—they are the easiest thing in the world to sew. I love to make them out of old white cotton bed sheets. If you don't have a stash of vintage cotton, think about shopping the sale racks. One twin flat sheet will yield three pillowcases. (I once bought a king-size flat sheet, 250 TC, on sale at T.J. Maxx for $7.)

What other fabric would be good for pillowcases?

How about white damask tablecloths? Nobody I know actually uses them on their tables. We're terrified somebody will spill coffee or wine...and then, too, there's all that ironing. Most white damask tablecloths are neatly folded and carefully stored in drawers or linen closets. For decades. Therefore, they arrive at the Goodwill store in excellent condition. I am not suggesting that you cut up your personal family history, but I am suggesting that you go ahead and cut up some other family's heirloom tablecloth.

White damask tablecloths often show up at estate sales, garage sales, and auctions. There just isn't much demand for them. And make no mistake—damask is a beautiful luxury fabric, so why not make some elegant pillowcases for yourself or as a special gift?

Pillowcases are quick and easy to make. They're a great project for kids and teens to work on, too. Personalized pillowcases make a very special wedding gift. Here are directions for two methods. Remember—if you want to embellish the pillowcase, do it before you sew the sides together. (More about embellishment later on.)

No matter where you get your fabric—old or new—here are the general dimensions:

Size	Finished Size	Cut Two pieces of fabric/ or, cut one:	
Standard	20" x 30"	21" x 35"	42" x 35"
Queen	20" x 34"	21" x 39"	42" x 39"
King	20" x 40"	21" x 45"	42" x 45"

These dimensions allow for a 4" hem on the open end.

First Method

1) Cut one piece of fabric: 42" x 35" for a standard case.

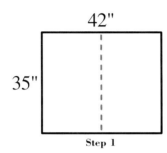

Step 1

2) Fold it, right sides together, and sew the bottom seam, and the side seam.

Step 2

3) Put in the 4" hem around the opening.

Step 3

Horizontal pillowcase

33

Second Method

1) Cut one piece of fabric 21" x 70".

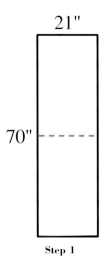

Step 1

2) Put right sides together, then sew the two long sides. The bottom of the case is the fold.

Step 2

3) Put in the 4" hem around the opening.

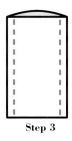

Step 3

Vertical pillowcase

Mary Mulari perfected this method because she loves to make pillowcases out of a twin flat sheet. She has devised this nifty layout so she can get three queen-size pillowcases out of one sheet (see illustration below). Smart, huh? With this layout method, Mary has a decorative hem on just one side of her pillowcase, but she has three pillowcases that match. Her Ralph Lauren twin flat sheet cost $8 on sale at Marshall's, whereas the matching set of queen-size pillowcases was $30 (and that was the sale price). The secret to Mary's success is that she uses the sheet's own decorative hem for one side of the opening of the pillowcase. The other side, she finishes off before sewing up the side seams. Great idea.

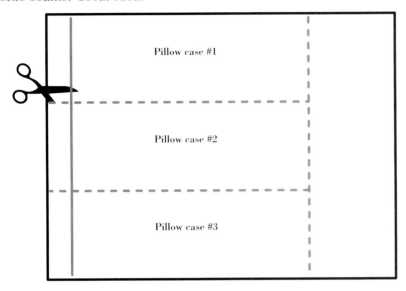

Twin flat sheet
66" x 96"

Here are some pillowcase examples from my Sewing Star Friends:

Sue Hausemann, hostess of "America Sews," sent me boxes of samples, including these two beautiful pillows. Doing just the opposite of what is expected, Sue used some brightly colored fabric for the cases, then chose a plain fabric for the border. Her embroidery decoration is really a stand-out and took only a few minutes to do.

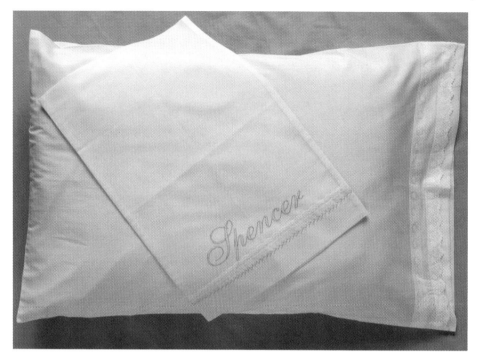

Debra Justice, known for her heirloom sewing classes, chose a fine-quality batiste for her delicate pillowcases. The pink case is simply finished off with some flat lace—and the small baby-blue case has her son's name, "Spencer," hand-stitched with a shadow-appliqué. The pillow that fits in this case has been passed down from mother through two baby boys…and I'm telling you, the little boy is just as sweet as the pillowcase.

Pamela Burke teaches classes on monogramming, both by hand and machine. Her stitching is so precise, it's hard for me to tell, but I'm pretty sure she did these by hand. Although she prefers a classy off-white thread on white fabric, for the purposes of photography, she used this subtle turquoise on elegant white linen cases.

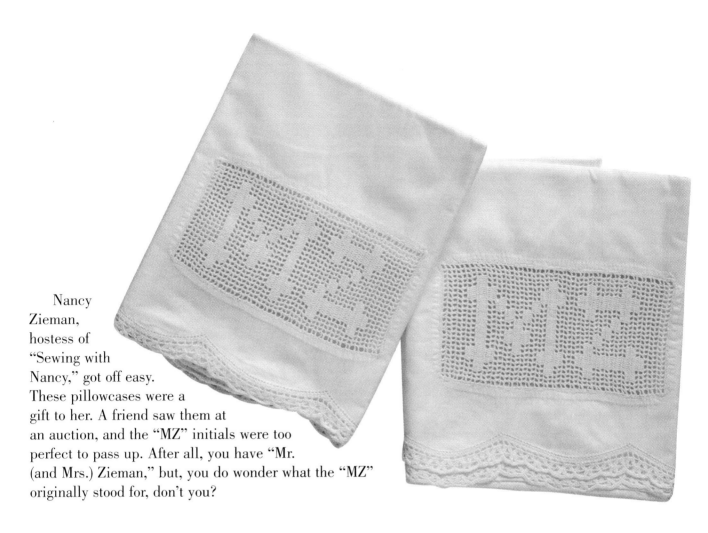

Nancy Zieman, hostess of "Sewing with Nancy," got off easy. These pillowcases were a gift to her. A friend saw them at an auction, and the "MZ" initials were too perfect to pass up. After all, you have "Mr. (and Mrs.) Zieman," but, you do wonder what the "MZ" originally stood for, don't you?

Joanne Ross made these pillows from a white damask tablecloth. Photographing the damask design in the fabric was difficult, but the moment you touch these pillowcases, you know what an elegant fabric this is. Joanne used white thread for the traditional elegant white on white. She combined embroidered flower stitches with an "RR" monogram.

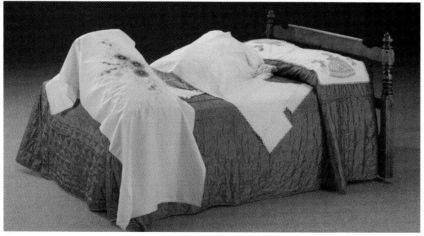

Flat Pillow Shams

Conventional "pillow shams" have never tripped my trigger. It seems like a lot of work to get the pillows in and out. Most people end up tossing them on the floor when they get into bed. However, I do understand the decorative element.

So, with pleasure, I revive an old bedding tradition—what I call a "flat sham." Also referred to as a "pillow shelf," it's simply a piece of embellished fabric that covers your pillows.

The example in the top-left photo of some big square redwork vintage flat shams belongs to Mary Mulari and has a very unusual matching bed banner. Isn't that a hoot? Her shams are 24" x 32". The banner above, with the words "Good Night," measures 18" x 48". What a wonderful and unique way to decorate your bed!

If you like the flat-sham idea, it's easy enough to make your own using modern-day embroidery, or maybe sewing a small doily onto a flat piece of beautifully hemmed fabric. Or, you may already own something that would work. Perhaps an old dresser scarf is long enough, like this poinsettia piece, middle photo, at left, my grandma made. Or you could cut a new one out of an old tablecloth.

Top bed: Mary Mulari's vintage redwork; middle bed: use a doily or tablecloth as a flat sham; bottom bed: several different flat shams laid out on top.

The bed in front of the clothesline, shown below, is actually made with a "summer set"; the flat sham is a separate piece. The quilted sham on top of the purple bed, in the bottom photo, is made from feed-sack calico fabric. In the close-up shot at right, you can see that the back of the sham is from "sugar sacks," which were meant to be disposable.

When your people lay their heads down at night, the last thing they see and feel and smell is the pillowcase. Make sure they know you cared enough to make it special for them. Their pillowcase should look beautiful, feel luxurious, and smell wonderful.

It's amazing this vintage piece survived in such great condition. You can still read the writing from the sacks.

Make special pillowcases and hang them outside to dry so they'll smell wonderful. If you can't do that, spray them with lavender water or store them in a drawer with a lavender sachet. At the end of the day, they will drift off to sleep, feeling loved. Isn't that the whole point?

Between The Sheets

When John and I got married in 1970, we bought one of those new-fangled, queen-size beds. Pretty avant-garde, eh? That was the first and last time we were ever on the cutting edge of anything. The guy who invented the queen-size bed should be a bizillionaire—everybody I know has one.

Two examples of boxed sheet sets from the 1950s, still wrapped in the original cellophane.

Of course, kids still living at home sleep in double beds. (Generally, the one that Grandma got rid of when she bought her new queen size.) Then, too, if you have a small apartment in New York City, like my friends Judy and Steve, you may have a double bed. And I can't forget my cousin Kim, who doesn't want to give up her floor space.

The point is, when vintage linens were being made, they were always for double beds. But according to my local bed-selling experts, today queen-size beds outsell double beds by at least seven to one. So, a big focus of this book is to modify those beautiful vintage "full-size" bed linens to fit on queen-size beds.

Dimensions for standard beds

Twin bed:	38" wide by 75" long
Extra-long twin:	38" wide by 80" long
Double bed:	54" wide by 75" long
Queen-size bed:	60" wide by 80" long
King-size bed:	76" wide by 80" long

When designing sheets for any bed, the key number is the *depth* of the mattress. This can vary a lot. The mattress we bought in 1970 was 10 inches deep. Today, if you buy a premium mattress with a pillow top, the depth could be 16 inches.

For the sake of clarity throughout the project sections of this book, let's establish some simple terminology:

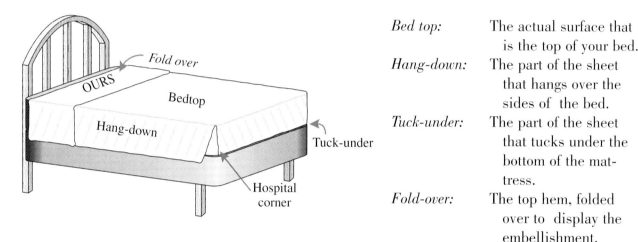

Bed top:	The actual surface that is the top of your bed.
Hang-down:	The part of the sheet that hangs over the sides of the bed.
Tuck-under:	The part of the sheet that tucks under the bottom of the mattress.
Fold-over:	The top hem, folded over to display the embellishment.

General Sewing Information

Modifying sheets—whether you are reworking vintage pieces or making new fitted sheets out of a bargain flat sheet from T.J. Maxx—I'm assuming 100 percent cotton. With that in mind, here are some guidelines to get you started:

- ✐ Set up your machine for a straight stitch, with a 2.5 stitch length.
- ✐ Sew with a good quality 100 percent cotton quilting thread (also in your bobbin).
- ✐ Start every project with a new standard-size #80 needle.

This is some of the easiest sewing in the world—all straight seams and long lines. Anybody with a basic sewing machine can get great results. It is not the least bit complicated. Trust me— your friends will act like you single-handedly launched the Space Shuttle.

With 100 percent cotton, you may "rip" the sheet, rather than cut it with a scissors. It's quick, easy, and finds the straight of grain. Old white cotton sheets are beautifully woven and hold up well to ripping. If you have a problem at this early stage, it could mean the sheet is worn out, and not worth the trouble to modify.

HIDDEN SEAM

They used to call this a double seam, or a French seam. I use my serger to make pillowcases or add extenders to sheets. But, if you're real picky, you may want to brush up on this classic old technique to hide the raw edges.

1) Sew a regular seam, wrong sides together (this could be serged).

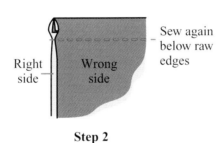

Step 1

2) Turn them over at the seam, so the right sides come together and the two raw edges are hidden; make another seam below the first, making sure no raw edge is visible on the outside of the seam (regular sewing machine).

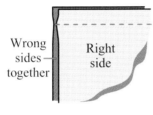

Step 2

3) If you like, you could now topstitch, which flattens the seam, and makes for a very elegant finished look.

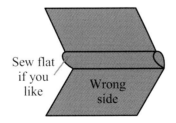

Step 3

How to Make a Sheet Extender

If you put a flat sheet made for a double bed (usually 81" x 102") on a queen-size bed, you would still have a 10-inch hang-down on each side of the bed, which is okay. The problem is with the tuck-under at the bottom of the bed. Although the queen bed is only 5" longer, I like to add at least 12" of fabric—I get a better tuck-under and an elegant fold-over.

FIRST METHOD

To modify a vintage sheet with an "extender":

1) Rip the bottom hem off the sheet.

2) Rip a 12-inch section off the bottom of a second flat sheet.

3) With right sides together, sew or serge the strip from the second sheet to the bottom of the sheet. To make the bed, put the serged seam on top so you can't feel it with your toes when you get in bed.

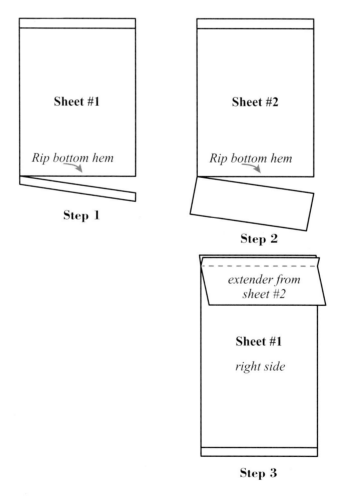

44

SECOND METHOD

For this two-tone variation, I ripped 12" off the top of a vintage yellow sheet and sewed it to the *top* of a white flat sheet. I embroidered "Mulari" in the center of the newly added yellow fold-down. This is a gift for my friend Mary, but she has to give it back every now and then for photography.

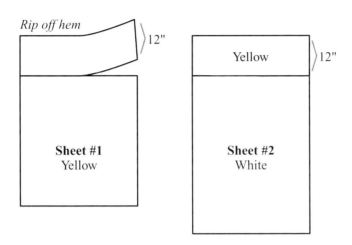

The top sheet has a 12-inch yellow "extension."

From this—two Queen flat sheets from the bargain bin.

Make a Fitted Sheet

This is a little trickier, but you will get raves when you give somebody a handmade set of sheets. They make a wonderful, unusual gift. You can start with brand new flat sheets, like these lavender queen-size flat sheets from Polo. I bought them off a clearance table at TJ Maxx for $10 each, and transformed them into a "set" that would cost $400.

The new lavender fitted sheet is 16" deep. After making the fitted sheet out of one of the flat sheets, I had a 4" strip of fabric leftover, enough to trim a pair of plain white pillowcases (vintage 100 percent cotton Duracale, still in the package—more Ritaluck). By cutting off the hem, adding the lavender fabric, then re-attaching the hem, the pillowcases became "queen size." This beautiful new set, below, complete with the "POLO" logo, became a very special wedding gift. You'll meet the new bride at the end of the book.

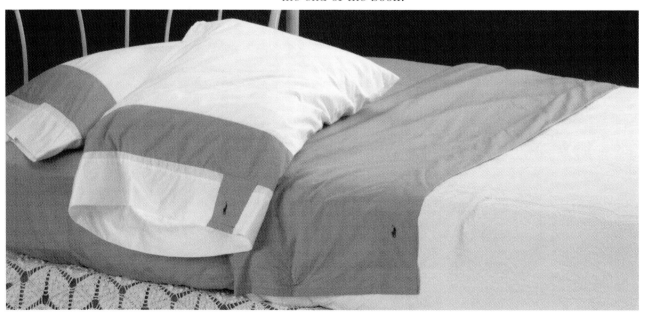

To this—a complete sheet set—fitted, flat, and newly trimmed pillowcases. I even salvaged the "Polo" logo.

1) Use a seam ripper to open up the deep hem at the top of the sheet.

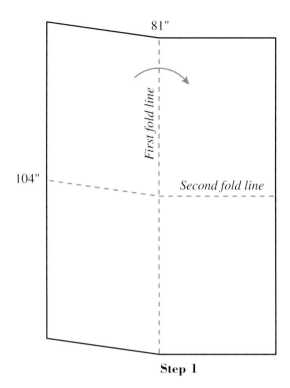

Step 1

2) Fold the sheet in half both ways to mark the absolute center point.

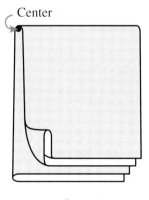

Step 2

3) From that center point, measure a length of 80" and a width of 60"—that will be the *top* of your bed sheet. At each corner, cut in 12" from all four sides to form the fitted corners.

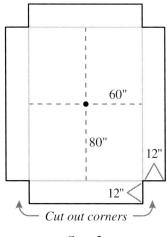

Step 3

4) Serge or sew the 12" edges, right sides together, to form the fitted corners.

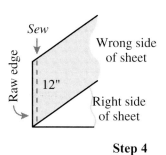

Step 4

5) Topstitch the seam allowance to the sheet for a finished look and extra strength.

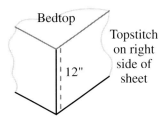

Step 5

6) Serge or sew 1/4" elastic around the top and bottom ends of the sheet, stretching the elastic as you stitch. You could turn the elastic and topstitch for a more finished look (I never do).

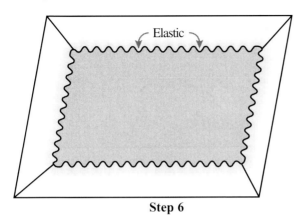

Step 6

Those are the basic instructions to make a fitted sheet for a standard queen-size mattress. **But not so fast!** The new mattresses are much deeper, so you need deeper sheets. But don't lose heart! It's not impossible. Even if you have a very thick mattress, with one of those new pillow tops, you can make a fitted sheet.

First of all, the top of a queen-size mattress is always 60" x 80". But it's the depth of your mattress that determines how deep the corners have to be—and that's the determining factor in your math calculations.

For example, if your mattress is 16" deep (and many of them are), you will need to add enough fabric to the sides of your vintage sheet to make it 94" x 114". Add the fabric first, before you cut out the corners.

In the photo at right, I added a contrasting printed fabric all around the vintage white flat sheet. Then, I cut in 16" from each side to form the fitted corners and proceed with the directions given. Get it? Your corners will be 16" deep instead of 12". That just means you have a way better mattress than I do. Lucky you!

Tip:
I like to use 1/4" lingerie elastic for my fitted sheets. It is very resilient and holds up well to repeated washings.

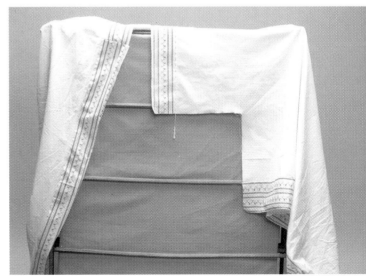

A second way to make the sheet fit the deeper mattresses is to add "flanges" of different fabrics, like this yellow sheet I made for Mary Mulari.

1) Cut the top white piece 60" x 80"

2) Add yellow pieces 17" deep on all four sides.

3) Cut out the corners and proceed as usual.

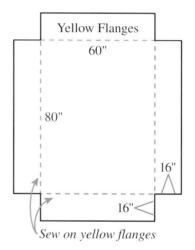

Sew on yellow flanges

One vintage yellow sheet provided enough fabric for the extender on the flat sheet AND the four sides for the new fitted sheet.

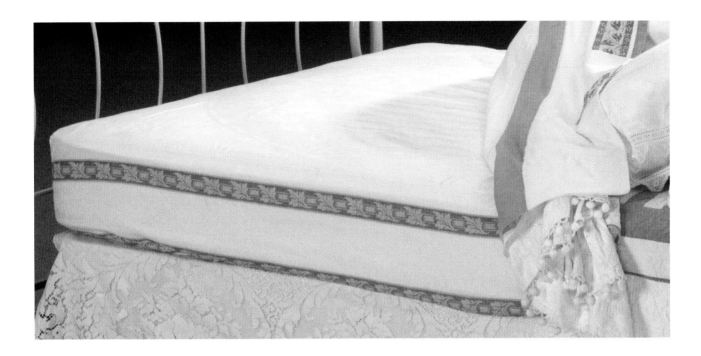

With the flanged method, it's possible to make a fitted sheet out of a damask tablecloth. This Bluebird bed, above, is one of my favorites. Although you can't see it, there is an elegant oval medallion pattern in the center of the sheet, as the bed top used to be a white damask tablecloth. The flanges of the sheet were made out of a vintage blue and white striped damask tablecloth. This bedding is the ultimate in luxury.

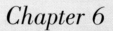

Chapter 6

The Thrill of the Frill

ow can something as basic as a flat sheet be considered elegant? First and foremost is the quality of the fabric. Luxurious sheets of yesteryear were 100 percent cotton with a high thread count or perhaps finely woven linen.

But in the good old days, the elegance of fine bed linen was conveyed by embellishment, and the primary area to decorate was always the hem.

In its heyday in the 1920s, the Naumkeag Steam Cotton Company had a huge work area called the "Hemming Room," where hundreds of young women worked at tables stacked high with machine-hemmed white sheets. Their job? Pull a few threads out to make a fancy drawn-thread hemstitch. The elegance was in the details.

But the most elaborate embellishments were applied after the sheet was purchased. Every household had different preferences or needlework skills. The homemaker might apply a simple crocheted trim. Wealthy families would have their servants embroider elaborate monograms. The embellishment was always placed in such a way that when the deep hem was folded down, that touch of elegance was revealed. The embellishment applied to the sheet would be duplicated on the pillowcases, making a "sheet set."

There were as many different ways to embellish bed linens as family recipes to make biscuits. The best thing about decorating sheets and/or pillowcases is that you are sewing less than 100 inches, so ANYBODY CAN DO IT. Everything in this chapter can be done by hand or with a sewing machine.

By now, you've seen the value of those boring old white cotton flat sheets your mother packed away 30 years ago. You've whitened them and brightened them. Time now to decorate them. But, if you don't have a stash of old white cotton sheets, go shopping! Look for 100 percent cotton sheets with a thread count of 200+. SUPIMA is the best. Be sure to check out the bargain bins for mismatched flat sheets. Remember—you can make a fitted sheet and/or pillowcases out of flat sheets, and with your newly embellished flat sheet, you'll have a "gift set."

Decorative Hems

As you can see in this picture of flour-sack pillowcases from the Little family, sewing on a calico hem was the complete decoration. It made a big difference and it couldn't have been easier.

Adding a completely new, deeper hem to a flat sheet, using contrasting or printed fabric, results in both a decoration and a sheet extender. You could also embellish the hem before you sew it on the sheet. Then, you could make pillowcases to match. The most important thing about this technique is that all the raw edges are concealed.

In the example, pictured above and at left, I used snowman fabric. My cousin Kim helped me do the photography for this book. We took all the outside pictures at her house, using her clothesline as a backdrop. She collects snowmen, and this sheet is all the payment she's gonna get.

Full size flat sheets are usually 81" x 101", but most printed fabrics are only 45" wide. That would create an unsightly seam in the middle of your pretty new hem, but you can eliminate that problem by creating a center medalli

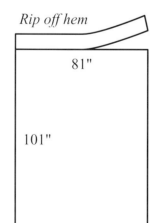

Rip off hem

81"

101"

DIRECTIONS FOR ADDING A DECORATIVE HEM (SNOWMAN SHEETS)

The project begins with a vintage flat sheet, cutting off the top hem.

1) The new contrasting hem (finished) will be 10" wide by 18" long. You need two pieces of Snowman fabric (to go on either side of the center medallion) 21" wide x 36" long.

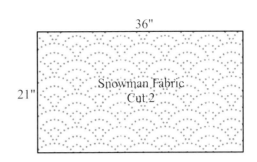

Step 1

2) Make the Medallion first. It will be 21" long and 10" wide. (If you want it bigger, make the side panels smaller.) Applique the snowman on the white fabric BEFORE joining with the two new snowman fabric pieces on each side. Be cautious about the placement. Remember, you will be folding the hem down.

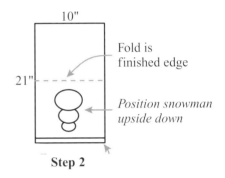

Step 2

3) Sew the snowman fabric onto each side of the center medallion. Now you have a new decorative hem.

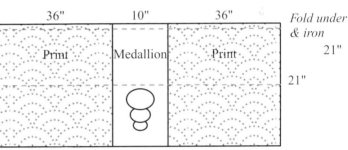

Step 3

4) With right sides together, sew the new hem piece onto the sheet, always starting in the center and sewing out to each side (to prevent puckers).

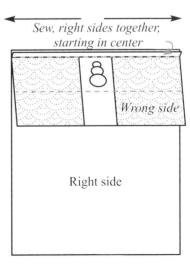

Step 4

Folded, right sides together

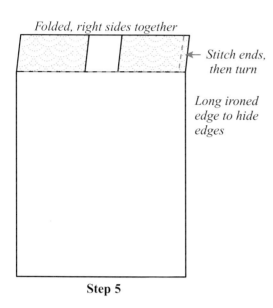

← *Stitch ends, then turn*

Long ironed edge to hide edges

Step 5

5) Iron a 1/2" seam along the unattached long edge of your new hem. Fold the new hem, right sides together, and stitch down each end. Then, turn the hem.

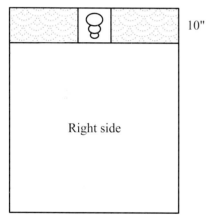

10"

Right side

Finished sheet

Step 6

6) The ironed-under hem is now on the back of your sheet, and should cover the raw edges of the new seam. Pin securely and topstitch with your machine or handstitch. Start in the center, and sew out to each side. (Use a matching thread in your bobbin, as this will show on the finished side of your sheet.

Now you have a beautiful new trimmed sheet with no exposed raw edges. You could add lace trim into the seam, or even a ruffle.

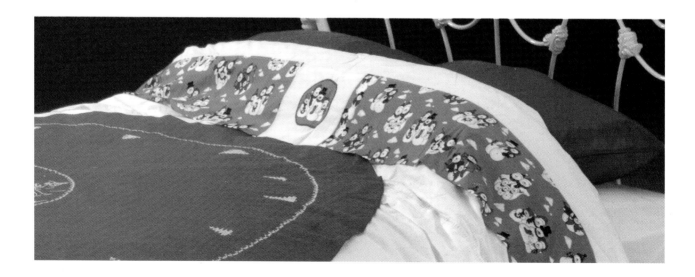

On this Bluebird bed, the new contrasting hem has a vintage towel, with the "R" monogram as a center medallion. This towel happened to be hanging on the line during our cover shoot. Recognize it? That plain little towel became a fabulous new top sheet, and a vintage damask tablecloth became a fitted sheet to match.

The Bluebird quilt was another auction find: only $40. Yeah, I know…Ritaluck strikes again. Even I'm surprised at how beautifully it all goes together.

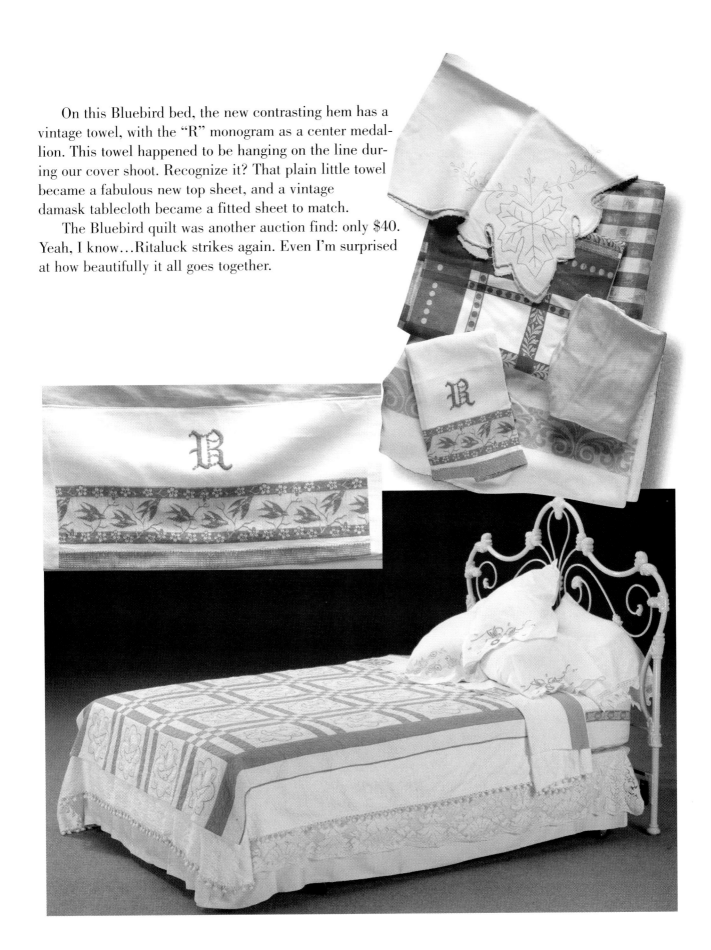

Embroidery By Hand

Embroidery was one of the most common ways to decorate sheets and pillowcases. Again, the linens of farm families would have been embroidered with colorful flowers or bird designs, while the upper classes would have used white thread on white fabric. This is a picture of some embroidered pillowcases, many of them with crocheted edges. All of them began as "pre-stamped" pillowcases, which are still available today. In the photo at left, you'll see some pillowcases that are stamped, but not yet embroidered. Maybe they'll be my winter project.

When I was a child, my Grandma Dodds taught me how to embroider. We would sit on her front porch for hours. We talked about everything under the sun during those lazy afternoons. I still think it's a wonderful way to spend time with your daughters, granddaughters, and nieces. (Yes, I know we're leaving the boys out—they're just too busy pretending to be professional wrestlers.) This could easily turn into a lifetime hobby for them and a worthwhile, relaxing pastime.

I enlisted the help of Pamela Burke to edit this chapter. Pam teaches classes on embroidery and monogramming all over the world, and her depth of knowledge is unique and impressive.

Pam says you only need to master five basic stitches to do beautiful embroidery and monogramming. She recommends: outline stitch, cross-stitch, lazy daisy stitch, satin stitch, and chain stitch. To get started, you may want to do research at your local library or purchase a hand-embroidery book.

Pam suggests that before you stick a needle into your beautiful soon-to-be-embellished sheet, you practice embroidery on

This is a picture of some embroidered pillowcases, many of them with crocheted edges. All of them began as "pre-stamped" pillowcases, which are still available today.

muslin dishtowels, which are inexpensive yet useful. If your beginning work isn't great, your pots and pans won't care.

The advantage of hand embroidery is that you can carry it with you and do something productive during those odd moments—while you wait in the dentist's office or watch your kid's soccer game (you can only embroider if he's on the bench). It's easy to carry a pillowcase and if you're working on a sheet, you can carry the hem separately, to be sewn onto the big sheet when your design is complete. My friend Judy loves to crochet. She takes it with her every place she goes. It is amazing how many afghans she makes while sitting in meetings or riding in a car.

Here are Pam's five favorite ways to transfer a pattern onto your fabric:

- Draw the pattern on the fabric using a #2 pencil.

- Use tracing paper to copy a design.

- Aunt Martha's embroidery transfers. They're inexpensive and easy to find.

- An iron-on transfer pencil. Pam likes the ones made by W.H. Collins because they wash out easily. Follow the instructions on the back of the package to make your transfer.

- Go to your local copy shop. Make a copy of any design you like. Put the copied design face down on fabric and press with a hot iron for 15 seconds. (The design will "mirror" as you iron it on.) Grandma would have loved Kinko's. The black lines will eventually wash out, but it's still a good idea to use a design with fine lines that the embroidery floss will cover.

Pam Says
Wrap the Hoop:

Cut bias strips of soft cotton fabric 1-1/4" wide. Begin close to the tightening screw. Put a dab of stick glue onto the fabric and finger press it into place. Wrap the entire hoop with one light layer of fabric. If you run out of fabric, glue another piece onto the place where you ran out, and continue wrapping. When you come to the other side of the tightening screw, whip the fabric into place with a needle and thread or glue it. Be sure that the end is on the outside of the hoop. Now, repeat the process with the inside hoop, being certain that the ending is on the inside of the hoop. This process gives your hoop better gripping power so the fabric will stay tight while you are embroidering.

Embroidery By Machine

For the last 10 years, sewing machine manufacturers have been focusing big time on machine embroidery. You can see from the samples on the rack above how incredible these machine stitches are—and it's unbelievably easy to obtain these professional results.

My friend Maureen Van Loon, pictured below, is 80 years old and a total whiz-bang with machine embroidery. I called Maureen when I needed help making samples for this book. She tells everybody to "buy the best sewing machine you can afford—no matter how old you are." Her attitude is that you're never too old to deserve the best and she's earned it!

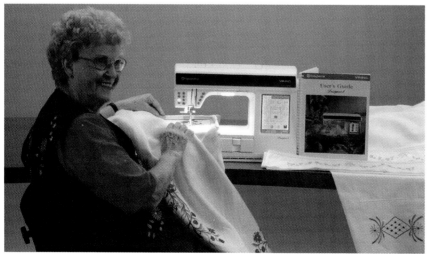

The embroidery for the sheet hems was done on a nice big piece of plain white cotton (out of my stash of white vintage sheets). *After* Maureen did the embroidery, she cut the hem to the correct width, and sewed it onto the new white sheet. That way, if you mess up the embroidery, you haven't ruined the entire sheet. Also, it's easier to hoop the project *before* it's attached to the sheet.

The biggest benefit of doing the embroidery first, then adding it to the sheet, is that after you sew it on (using the directions for the Decorative Hem), you have hidden the "back side."

The sheet above is a gift for my friend, Marion, who has taken back her maiden name of "Abel." The beautiful embroidery design was developed by Maureen, but I take credit for the words. The sheet says, *"Willing & Abel."* (I just crack myself up.)

Here are Maureen's tips for successful machine embroidery:

- Carefully consider the location and size of your design.
- Use two layers of stabilizer.
- Hoop your project securely.

Most of the work is in the preparation of the project. The embroidery itself only takes the machine a few minutes.

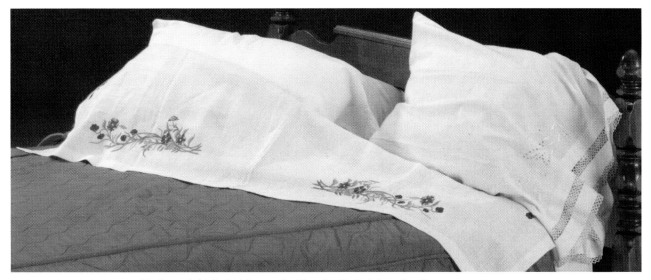

We dressed this bed with an embroidered tablecloth from Sue Hausmann.

This Patriotic sheet is a combination of machine embroidery and contrast hems. Maureen first embroidered the American flags on a big piece of white cotton. Then, she created the red, white, and blue fabric by cutting strips and serging them together. After assembling the hem in the right order, she joined the colorful new hem to a vintage white sheet, using the technique described earlier, concealing all the raw edges and the backside of the embroidery.

Talk to someone in your favorite sewing machine store who is knowledgeable about machine embroidery. Reputable machine dealerships offer wonderful classes and their staff can help you to achieve beautiful results.

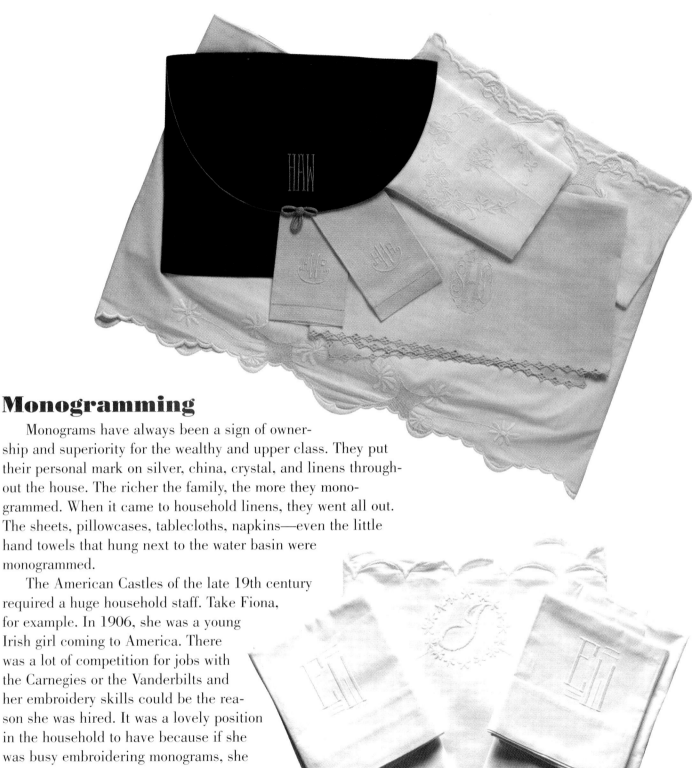

Monogramming

Monograms have always been a sign of ownership and superiority for the wealthy and upper class. They put their personal mark on silver, china, crystal, and linens throughout the house. The richer the family, the more they monogrammed. When it came to household linens, they went all out. The sheets, pillowcases, tablecloths, napkins—even the little hand towels that hung next to the water basin were monogrammed.

The American Castles of the late 19th century required a huge household staff. Take Fiona, for example. In 1906, she was a young Irish girl coming to America. There was a lot of competition for jobs with the Carnegies or the Vanderbilts and her embroidery skills could be the reason she was hired. It was a lovely position in the household to have because if she was busy embroidering monograms, she couldn't be hauling out the chamber pots. (If I were Fiona, I would have encouraged the family to monogram their underwear.)

Through the years, the popularity of monograms has ebbed and flowed. Today they are definitely back in fashion. Women are no longer waiting to use monograms until they get married, either. So— go for it. A hundred years ago, a young girl's hope chest would be complete long before she met her Prince

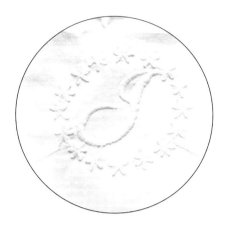

Charming. The elegant bed linens she brought into the marriage would have her maiden name initials and her husband's were added on top of her monogram.

The current style of letter placement, in vogue for the last century, is the initial of the last name placed in the center of a three-letter monogram. The centered initial is generally slightly larger than the flanking letters. The initial of the first name is placed to the left, and the middle name initial to the right. My name is Rita Kay Farro. So, my monogram would be "RFK." Often families chose to simply use the first initial of their last name. The sheet at left, with the letter "J," is an example of this tradition. Today, it's acceptable for women to use the initial of their first name. Whenever I find a vintage piece with an "R," I am delighted.

If you like monograms, go to the library or your local sewing store and get a book on the subject. There are hundreds of lettering styles available, and many different stitches. A source for wonderful letter styles are the fonts on your computer. Think about all the lettering styles available. Print off several that you like in large sizes, try sizes up to 70 or 80 points.

MONOGRAM BY HAND

Pam offers these basic instructions: Use one or two strands of embroidery floss and a #10 embroidery needle. She recommends a good brand of English needles such as John James or Richard Hemming.

▨ Draw the monogram onto a piece of tracing paper, turn it over, and trace the monogram on the backside of the design with an iron-on transfer pencil. Pam likes the W.H. Collins brand because they are bright, yet wash out easily.

▨ Stiffen your fabric with spray starch. (Fiona would have loved that stuff.)

▨ Hoop the area you're working on. (Check Pam's instructions for hoop preparation.)

▨ Begin by sewing in base or padding stitches, the easiest one is the chain stitch. These stitches provide depth and regularity to the finished monogram.

▨ Over sew the padding stitches with a satin stitch.

▨ A knot in the thread is not a good method to secure the

thread; rather, backstitch a couple of stitches before beginning the satin stitch. Knotted thread has a tendency to crawl up through the satin stitches when it is laundered.

Like everything else in life, you'll get better with practice.

MONOGRAM BY MACHINE

Home sewers now have unlimited access to alphabet styles. The general rules of placement still apply. The biggest decision you'll have when monogramming your new bed linens with your embroidery machine is whether to use white or colored thread. Again, your personal taste is all that matters. Pam prefers an off-white thread when working on white fabric—very subtle, yet classy.

When doing machine monogramming, Pam's choice for thread is Mettler cotton mercerized thread size 30/2. She says, "The natural soft luster of this thread never seems to diminish. As it is laundered, it develops a soft sheen. Use Mettler cotton mercerized 60/2 thread for bobbin thread, matching the color of the top thread. The look will be incredible."

Her second choice is polyester embroidery thread. It retains a lovely look over many washes and is quite durable. It does not have the same look as cotton, so test to make sure you like it. Mettler makes a polyester sewing thread called Metrosene. It will match most embroidery thread colors. Use that in your bobbin for excellent results.

In Pam's opinion, "Rayon thread is the least acceptable thread choice for machine monogramming on linens. With multiple washings, the color fades. Linens have a very long life expectancy and are laundered much more than clothing. Rayon thread is wonderful when used for the type of embellishment it is designed for."

A sheet is an ordinary element of our everyday lives. That's what I love about it. An embellished sheet set is a unique gift that will become a personal good luck talisman for your friends and family. Thanks to Pam, I'm confident that even a virgin sewer could buy a flat sheet, plan an embellishment, and get beautiful results the first time out. Decorating bed linens is a very simple, almost forgotten, art form. The time is right to bring it back.

The decorative hem also serves as a sheet extender.

Chapter 7

Skirting The Issue

The bed skirt is a seriously overlooked, underrated element of
an elegant bed. The bed skirt becomes especially
important if you have a queen-size bed and are using vintage linens or
bedspreads and quilts that were originally made to fit double beds.

This red and white tablecloth became a spectacular bed skirt. The tablecloth was laid open on top of the boxspring and the mattress keeps it in place. How easy is that?

Picking just the right bed skirt can make the whole bedroom come together. Remember—if your bed has a footboard, you only need a bed skirt with two sides. That's the beauty part of creating your dream bed. The linens should fit your taste *and* your furniture.

You can buy two basic types of bed skirts: ruffled or tailored. Both are widely available, usually for a reasonable price. You can also make your own and there are many books and patterns on the market to guide you.

But I want to show you unusual ways to dress your bed with a new skirt. Things you may not have thought of before, using treasures you may already own, like the tablecloths shown here.

I bought this bed skirt at the Goodwill store for $5, along with the matching custom-made pillows. More Ritaluck.

In the first photograph, you'll see the custom designer technique called "a continental shelf." Instead of sewing the "ruffle" directly onto the bedtop, you add a 3-inch edge of the decorator fabric. This detail is important if you tuck your bedspread. Also, if the mattress moves slightly, you will not see the unsightly boxspring top.

In the photo below, you can see how this gorgeous bed skirt made it possible to use the simple white bedspread (only a double size) on this queen-size bed Note that we boxed the corner of the bedspread. That gives it a nice tailored look.

Non-Sewing, Non-Traditional Bed Skirts

One of the main purposes of a bed skirt is to hide the unsightly box spring. The easiest way is to simply cover your box spring with a fitted sheet. One of those ritzy mail-order catalogs features a bed with an orange fitted sheet on the box spring, and a pink fitted sheet on the actual mattress. Very sophisticated and chic.

Here are three non-sewing techniques for putting a skirt on your bed. Remember, this is an area that gets no wear and tear. If everything is going well, the bed skirt never actually comes into contact with the human occupying the bed.

- 🕮 <u>Carpet tape.</u> The wide, sticky-on-both-sides variety. Apply it directly to the top edge of the box spring.
- 🕮 <u>Velcro.</u> With the sticky on the back, apply the hook tape on the upper edge of the box spring, and the loop tape on the skirt.
- 🕮 <u>Safety pins.</u> Duh. If I drew you a picture, you'd be insulted.

This elegant bed skirt below is simply a white damask tablecloth draped over the box spring. We used two different tablecloths and didn't even have to pin them to the box spring. We just tucked them in under the mattress.

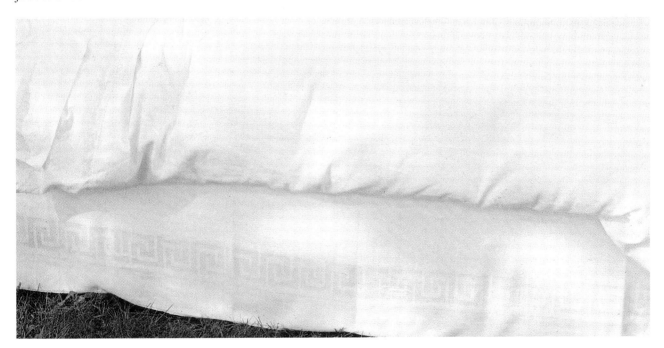

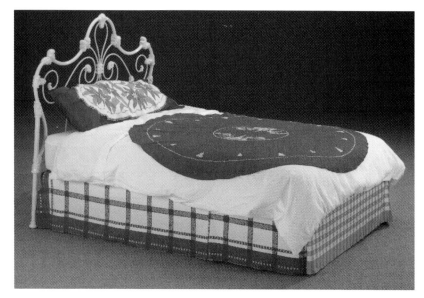

The tablecloths can be totally different. For this Christmas bed, we used a red and white tablecloth and a green and white tablecloth. Perfect.

For one of my favorite beds in this book, in the photo below, patriotic tea towels were just tucked between the mattress and box spring— to layer on top of the plain navy blue bed skirt. Nothing could be easier.

For a more elegant layered look, put a lace tablecloth on top of your existing bed skirt. It will be displayed and enjoyed, yet be safe from wine or food spills. On this bed, we put the lace on top of a purple satin bedspread.

For an elegant tone-on-tone look, you could put the lace on top of a white damask tablecloth, as was done for this Bluebird bed.

Everybody I talked to had a great idea for an original bed skirt. I didn't know my friends and family had such wonderful imaginations. Here are some of the best ideas. You'll probably come up with lots of your own. Go for it!

- Grass skirting
- Plastic racing flags banner
- Fringed denim
- Vintage doilies or handkerchiefs
- Christmas twinkle lights
- Red/white/blue patriotic buntings
- Bandannas or napkins, cornered
- Shamrock place mats

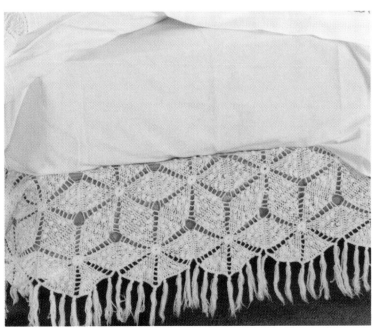

Lace alone makes a romantic bed skirt.

71

Chapter 8

'Tis The Season: Seasonal and Personalized Bedding

My Mom made her bed the exact same way every single day for 40 years, using the same white-fringed cotton bedspread. Actually, every ten years or so, she would buy a new one, but they all looked the same to me. My mother never heard of a bed skirt. As far as she was concerned, "duvet" was a suspicious-sounding French word.

After I married in 1970, I did the same thing. We received a blue-and-white-fringed cotton bedspread as a wedding gift, which I used every day for three years.

In 1973, I bought a yellow quilted bedspread to match the bedroom walls of our new house. The day we moved, I took my old bedspread to the Goodwill Store. I certainly didn't see the need for two different bedspreads.

"Seasonal" bedding was not a concept I had yet embraced.

However, as my collection of vintage linen grew, changing the bed dressing with the seasons became a very enjoyable aspect of my obsession.

In the winter, we sleep under a wool batt duvet. The duvet cover is crisp white cotton I bought in Ireland.. During the Christmas season, I use the poinsettia dresser scarf, seen above, Aunt Rozella gave me. Her mother, my Grandma Dodds, made this nearly 50 years ago.

In the summer, our bed is made up with a thin cotton flannel blanket, and a lightweight cross-stitch cotton quilt my Mother made for me. A work of art, my Mom's quilt belongs on a bed.

This cross-stitch quilt my mother made is a work of art.

My sheets? The same year round: 100 percent cotton, always white, usually embroidered or tatted. I rotate my four or five sheet sets. When I get new ones, my old favorites are given away as gifts.

For those in-between seasons—spring and fall—I love to change my bed dressing, depending on my auction finds. I am anxious to sleep in the Bluebird bed, on P. 75, we created for this book. What a great spring bed!

You may not want to re-dress your family beds four times a year, but you could; or, do it twice a year. That's the whole point. Rotate your best stuff—get it back onto the bed where it belongs. Why not use the seasons as an excuse to do that?

Since God created air conditioning, we don't have to suffer through the heat of summer anymore, but I still love the idea of a summer bed. It's my substitute for the spring cleaning my grand-mother used to do. She would spend a week cleaning the house: packing away winter clothes, taking carpets outside to hang on the lines so the dust could be beaten out of them, airing out rooms, washing windows, turning mattresses, and putting away the heavy wool quilts. I just change the dressing on my bed.

The bed featured at the beginning of this chapter is a won-

derful vintage "summer set" for a double bed and one of my most prized possessions, a perfect example of Ritaluck.

On a beautiful June day, my cousin Jackie and I ended up, quite by accident, at a big household auction in Belmont, Wisconsin. As we approached the big old house on Belmont's Main Street, every inch of the spacious front yard was covered with a lifetime's accumulation of household belongings. Rows of couches and bedroom furniture sat next to appliances and garden equipment.

A long set of tables was covered with the 50-year assortment of household linens—towels, sheets, rugs, pillows, quilts, and mattress pads. Suddenly I knew how that guy must have felt when he found gold in California. Jackie got a bidding number. We were #165.

Our first buried treasure was a pristine white cotton full-size flat sheet in beautiful condition with a scalloped edge across the top, white embroidered flowers, and the monogrammed letter "J," shown at right. The sheet even had a beautiful little drawn thread hemstitching detail on the bottom hem (which I have never seen). When Jackie saw it, she broke out in a huge grin. After waiting most of the afternoon, Jackie got that sheet for only $2.50.

This Bluebird bed is perfect for spring.

In a huge pile of tablecloths, I discovered an embellished summer coverlet. I knew it was a bed coverlet because the lace edging was only on three sides. But the matching flat sham (which I knew must exist) was not with it. On another table—yippee kayee—I found the sham in a pile of dresser scarves. I knew this set would be perfect for my Bed Book. It is in spectacular condition—like it's never been used, much less laundered. My heart beat a lot faster.

The ringman held up my reunited summer set. The bidding started at $5 and two women were going at it fast and furious. They both seemed determined. My heart sank. I had never seen a set like this—and I soooo wanted to buy it.

The two warring women flew past $50. Maybe I wouldn't even get a chance to bid. When the auctioneer called for the $75 bid, the first bidder shook her head no. I forced myself to wait for just a moment and the second bidder thought she won.

The auctioneer called again for $75. Then, I whistled in my bid. Apparently, nobody does loud finger whistles in Wisconsin. The whole crowd turned to look at me. The auctioneer was pleased to have a third bidder. I was now in at $75. As I'd hoped, the $70 bidder was taken aback. She looked in my direction and hesitated.

The auctioneer pronounced "SOLD"…and I held up my number. I bought the summer set on one bid of $75. I don't know how long I'd been holding my breath.

Although originally made for a double bed, this set, now known as "The Belmont Set" looks perfect on this queen-size bed, with a lace tablecloth bed skirt.

You could make a summer set; or, you could just go shopping in your cedar chest for a vintage tablecloth to display on your bed.

Maybe you have a round tablecloth that you love, but no round tables! This small square tablecloth, at right, with the extraordinary yellow stitching, is perfect to decorate my bed. Last year, I used the bright red Christmas tablecloth with the delicate white cross-stitching. Simply display the tablecloths on the center of the bed. Of course, you could stitch them on your duvet cover if you'd like, or use buttonholes to attach them.

Depending on how you feel about holidays, you can carry this themed idea to the hilt. I think Christmas bedding, right, is a great idea, but maybe you'd like to do something special for St. Patrick's Day or Halloween.

Personalizing bedding can be a real kick for kids, too. Everybody knows that you should never personalize child's clothing, since putting his or her name on a shirt or a jacket makes it too easy for a stranger to act familiar. But, a child's bed is a completely acceptable and safe place to personalize—and kids love seeing their name on things.

When my nephew, Jeff, was one-year-old, I made him a pillowcase with J-E-F-F spelled out in big letters. I wish I had made one for all of my 20+ nieces and nephews, but I didn't. Another one of life's little moments I missed.

Looking back, I can't imagine what could have been more important at the time.

Let the kids get involved in creating their own dream beds. My son, Ross, would choose a Cubs baseball theme every time. Boys are usually left out when it comes to their bedding, but they should be encouraged to participate. Boys especially need a soft place to fall into. What better place than their own bed?

T-Shirt Quilt

This may be a quilt your child will treasure 50 years from now. In this case, all the T-shirts were acquired from races young Dustin ran in. Maureen Van Loon began by cutting 16" squares out of the T-shirt fronts. You could sew the squares to each other, making long strips, then sew the strips together; or, you could take a little more time and use joining strips. In this example below, Maureen used a joining strip between all the shirt squares, which brings the colors together with the border. (She also used a lightweight fusible interfacing on the T-shirt fabric to keep it from stretching.)

Elliott's Memory Quilt

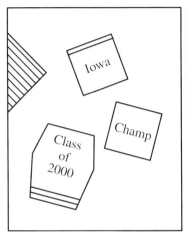

Step 1

1) Start with a flat sheet. Place your most important pieces on the sheet, and straight stitch around the edges.

2) Lay another piece on top, right sides together. Sew and flip (covering the raw edges). Sew and flip over and over, as illustrated.

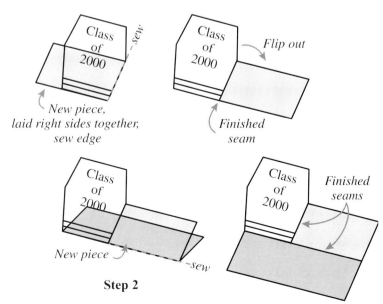

Step 2

3) Keep building around the most important pieces until the sheet is completely covered.

4) Place another sheet on top of the Memory quilt, right sides together, and sew all around, leaving a 12" hole in the bottom for turning.

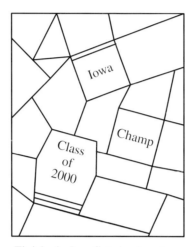

Finished - Lay flat sheet on top, sew around edges, leaving 12" hole for turning.

Step 3

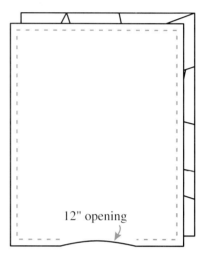

12" opening

Plain sheet on top, right side together

Step 4

5) Turn, just like a pillowcase, and whipstitch the opening.

6) Iron the edges, and topstitch.

7) I pinned the quilt and the backing together, and added small embroidered satin "hearts" every 10" or so, in a random pattern.

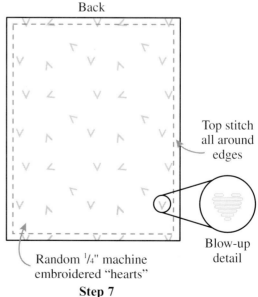

Back

Top stitch all around edges

Blow-up detail

Random ¼" machine embroidered "hearts"

Step 7

80

I gave the quilt on the bed above to my
son, Elliott, for his 18th birthday. It has a piece from my Dad's
bib overalls and my Mom's gingham apron; the shirt John was
wearing on our first date; his brother Ross' favorite baseball
team; and the T-shirts Elliott won in shooting competitions, as
well as the red satin jacket he wore on his first day of kindergarten. He wasn't very impressed with this gift when he was 18
years old, but he has slept under it every day since. I think one
day, maybe when he's 50, he'll suddenly look at his familiar old
quilt and know how much love went into making it.

I simply adore the idea of bedding with a message. This vin-
tage sheet, below, is probably close to 100 years old. The words,
"God Natt—Sof Godt" are crocheted into needle lace. I think it's
Swedish for "Good Night, Sleep Well." Of course, a simple
"Sweet Dreams" would be perfect.

After we sisters took our trip to Ireland, I wanted to embroider "Cead Mile Failte" onto sheets for all of us. It's the Gaelic greeting which means, "A thousand welcomes." But my husband felt that was not a good message to put on sheets.

Oprah loves the story of *The Wizard of Oz*. If she was a personal friend of mine (don't I wish), I would make her a set of sheets that said, "The Power is Within You."

There are the obvious things to put on sheets and pillowcases. "His and Hers," "Mr. and Mrs." If you make it yourself, personalized bedding can have a little zing. My cousin, Kim, is married to Bill Fitzgerald. How about a top sheet with "Fitzgerald" on it—and matching pillowcases that say, "Kim" and "Him."

Below is a picture of a sheet I designed for my friends, Judy and Steve. Judy taught English for 30 years, and her husband, Steve, is a very successful lawyer. They're an amazing couple by any standard, and they are both blind. But after you spend five minutes in a room with them, you forget that fact. Judy edited this book for me (several times). She is a wonderful editor and catches words even spell check misses. She and Steve recently purchased a home in Benicia, California. Steve is the master of bad puns—and his first comment was that if they got the house, they would officially be "The Benician Blinds." I groaned, too. But you've got to admit, he's pretty funny.

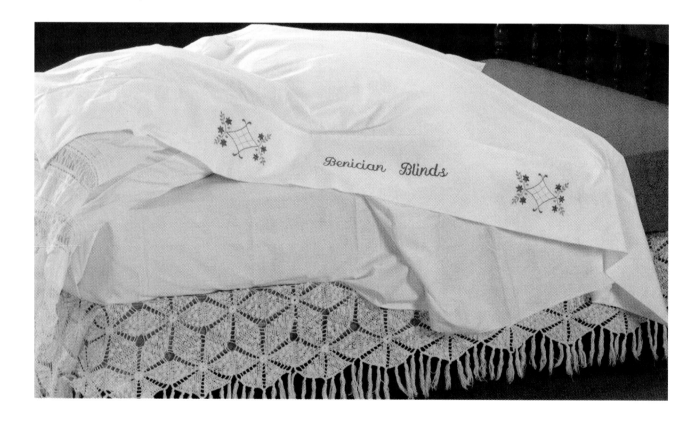

Chapter 9

Take Cover

*B*ed fashions, like all other trends, come and go. And, just like the clothes you wear, what you put on your bed is a matter of personal taste. That's the whole point of this book: Dressing your bed to reflect what you love and making it your own special sanctuary. Some people love the look of quilts; others prefer woven bedspreads. Comforters have made a big comeback in the last 10 years. So that's where I'm going to start. Puffy duvets...

You see them everywhere. They are easy and they serve two purposes: They keep you warm *and* they decorate the bed. To avoid confusion, as far as I'm concerned, the words "comforter" and "duvet" are interchangeable. Comforters come in all shapes and sizes. They can be filled with polyester, feathers, white goose down, or wool batting. But, like everything else you put on your bed, all duvets are *not* created equal. There are *huge* differences.

Polyester

There are many polyester comforters available on the market today, especially at discount department stores. Polyester is *always* part of those "bed in a bag" deals. These comforters are usually sold already covered with decorator fabric. They are inexpensive and easy to care for. My son, Ross, took one with him to college. I also have one on the porch for the dog to sleep on. So, now you know how I feel about polyester. It's good enough for college students and/or pets, and also perfectly fine for camping.

The Lowdown on Down

My Grandma Little always made feather pillows. When she sold feathers from her geese and ducks, way back then—they didn't actually separate the feathers from the down—it was all referred to as *pin feathers*. Grandma called this bit of extra income her "pin money." But today, at the factory, feathers are separated from down using a blower/sorting process.

I've slept on the same feather pillow for 30 years, but I can't get a good night's sleep under a down comforter. After 20 minutes, I feel like my hair is on fire. Again, this bedding thing is a matter of your own personal taste. So here's what I've learned about buying and caring for goose down.

Down is the very soft, shaftless clusters from the breast and underbelly of ducks and geese. Duck down can have a musty odor, even when new, so it's cheaper than goose down. Down clusters do not have hard, spiny feather quills. It can take 30 mature geese to yield a pound of down. In 1998, the U.S. imported 78 million pounds of feathers; 65 percent of the world's supply of "feathers and down" comes from China.

HOW TO SHOP FOR DOWN

There's good news and bad news with law labels. The bad news is that no penalty applies when manufacturers are dishonest about their contents. The good news is that housewives who have ripped off those labels with "penalty of law" warnings don't have to worry about going to jail.

"White goose down" on a label used to mean a minimum of 70 percent down. That's not true anymore—and without clear FTC regulations, you really don't know what you're getting. The feather industry uses the measurement of Filling Power to indicate the ability to create insulating space with minimum weight. The best high-quality down has a Filling Power of 600 or even 700 cubic inches per ounce, whereas the best feathers would have a Filling Power of 350 or less.

Buying a new white goose-down comforter is one of those "you get what you pay for" things. Small goose feathers sell for less than $2 a pound, whereas high-quality goose down sells for almost $80 for the same amount. So, to get the real thing, you *will* have to pay.

Down/Feather Care Instructions

Down can be dry cleaned or washed. Geese wore these feathers in all kinds of weather—including rain and snow—so water won't damage them, whereas, some dry-cleaning solutions can ruin the natural oils that provide bounce and loft. So washing is the preferred option. But before laundering, check the fabric covering. It should be strong, with no thin spots. Be sure to check for holes or rips in the seams. Check it out very carefully before proceeding. Otherwise, you risk a feather blizzard in your laundry room. These instructions are for one comforter or two pillows:

1. Start your washing machine and fill with hot water. Add one-half cup detergent or soap. Run the machine for two minutes to completely dissolve the soap, then stop the machine.

2. Place the comforter (or two pillows) in the water and push under and squeeze out as much air as you can. Remember—down is very buoyant and floats high on top of water (this is why ducks and geese have down and chickens don't). It doesn't want to get wet, so you will have to push down and squeeze until it's saturated. Permit the comforter to soak for at least an hour. (Pillows should soak for two hours.) This is the hardest part of the job—if your comforter or pillows weigh four pounds, it's like trying to drown 120 geese. You may have to weigh them down with plastic bottles filled with water to get them completely wet. Squeeze out the air again.

3. Start the machine and complete the washing cycle. Run your washing machine for one extra rinse cycle or two. *Rinse out all of the soap residue.*

4. Place the wet comforter or pillows into your dryer and set it on high. You can add a clean sneaker or new tennis balls to punch the down comforter or pillows as they get tossed about. Monitor very carefully. Every 15 minutes, remove the items and shake vigorously in all directions, then place back in dryer. Repeat this until your comforter (or pillow) is light and fluffy. After two hours in the dryer, I like to hang it outside in the sun to complete the drying process. Cradle the comforter or pillows on top of a sheet, hung between two clotheslines. The fresh outdoorsy smell will be intoxicating.

Mildew is the only enemy down has, so make sure your comforter or pillows are completely dry. The length of time required depends on the weight of your feathers/down.

The Other Natural Comforter

Maybe you had a bad experience with goose down. Perhaps you get overheated, or you got feathers when you paid for down. Maybe you just don't like buying a product that is imported from China. There is an excellent natural alternative grown, harvested, and made in the good old USA. Something old that is new again: 100 percent natural wool batting from sheep. Surprised? Just hang with me for a minute here.

Mary Mulari lives so far north she doesn't even have central air conditioning. She said, "Rita, you cannot write a book about luxury beds and not talk about wool batts. In my opinion, the best blanket in the world is a hand-tied wool batt. Because it breathes, I sleep under mine all year around. It keeps me warm without ever overheating my body."

That overheating thing made sense. My husband, John, who is diabetic, often has night sweats sleeping under a goose-down duvet.

I started to do research about wool batts. It turns out, this is a very old thing which has never gone out of style in some parts of the world. It's still used in all parts of the northwoods of Minnesota and Canada and it's very popular in Australia and New Zealand. It is simply the wool from sheep. After the wool is sheared, it is "scoured," then it goes through a carding machine, which combs the wool into a beautiful, soft finished product called a "batt." The carding machines being used today were often manufactured at the turn of the century. After the wool has been carded, it is layered between two pieces of cheesecloth and hand-tied at intervals to keep it together. In the old days, women would quilt fabric right onto the wool batt. They would put up a quilting frame and make it a big social event. I'm going to show you a much easier, less time-consuming variation.

There are some mysterious properties to sheep's wool. For one thing, wool can absorb 30 percent of its weight in moisture and not feel wet to the touch. It is the ultimate in "wicking." And, amazingly, because of its ability to handle moisture, wool keeps sheep warm in winter and *cool* in summer.

My friend Val, who suffers from fibromyalgia, directed me to Web sites full of testimonials from people with arthritis and fibromyalgia who swear by sleeping on or under wool batt. They claim they are getting a good night's sleep for the first time in years because the wool eases their joint pain and discomfort. Even people who live in warm, humid climates were raving about their experiences with wool batt.

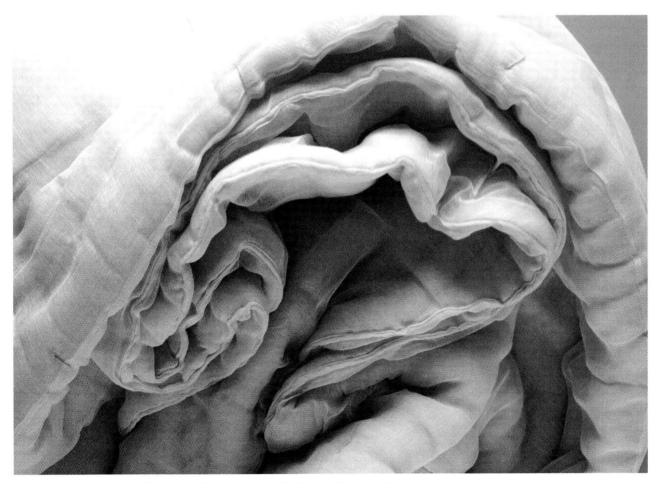

This is what wool batt looks like—combed sheep's wool inside hand-tied cheesecloth.

Well, I'd just better buy me one of those wool batts. The first person I experimented on was my sister Ronda. She has suffered from terrible hot flashes for years. She insists on sleeping with the windows wide open, even in the dead of winter. The family joke is that she doesn't turn her furnace on until there is skim ice in the toilet.

I bought a cheesecloth-covered wool batt and we used two white cotton sheets to make a cover for it. I figured Ronda could use it on her bed, inside a duvet cover, just like a white goose-down comforter (which she *dies* under).

Here's the amazing thing. From the very first night, Ronda slept all night *under* the wool batt. Her husband, Dean, called me the next morning. He was delighted. He was warm for the first time in years. After two months, Ronda made the observation that she wasn't waking up with headaches anymore.

By now, we were really excited. It was wonderful to discover something that has been around forever and bring it back into our lives by making it new again. For Christmas that year, we ordered six more wool batts and had some big parties at Ronda's house to assemble the comforters. The directions follow directly. Ronda's girls each got one (Amy and Nicole both suffer from terrible migraine headaches and we figured it couldn't hurt.)

My Aunt Ada suffers from arthritis. One day, as we were visiting, I could tell her hand hurt when air just hit it. I told her about wool and what I'd been reading on the Internet, then I suggested she stick her hand inside the wool batt pillow I had in the car (Yes! They make pillows now!). You should have seen the look on her face. But I insisted, and she took the pillow home with her (one end split open). That night she went to bed with her hand stuck inside the pillow, surrounded by sheep's wool. The next day, she called and said, "I thought you were nuts, Rita. But such a strange thing happened last night. My hand started to tingle and then I fell asleep. I didn't wake up for six hours and that hasn't happened in years. Usually the pain wakes me and I have to get up to take a pill."

Wow. Aunt Ada's experience with wool batt may not be typical; and, as this book goes to print, my family has been sleeping under wool batt for six months. But I can tell you we are getting the best sleep of our lives. Me with my hot flashes and John with his diabetes and cold feet. The wool batt seems to regulate both our body temperatures and I cannot tell you what a huge fan I am. Thanks again, Mary. Although you may not be able to find wool-batt comforters in your area, you can refer to the Resources page at the back of the book. If you sew, the cost will be far less than a real white goose-down comforter. Here are the directions to cover the cheesecloth hand-tied wool batting, thus turning it into a regular duvet.

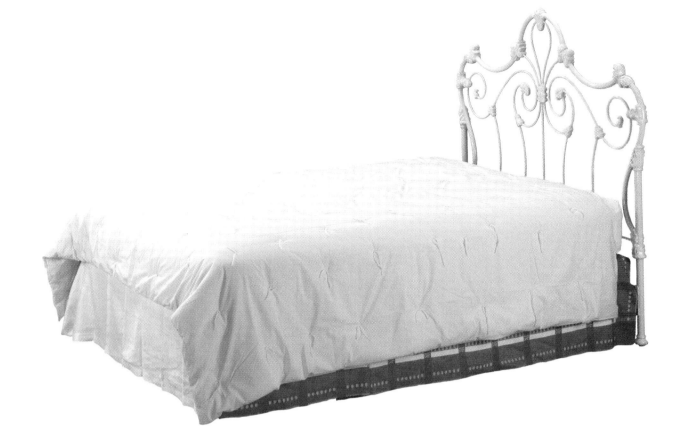

Cover Your Wool Batt

Your wool-batt comforter will arrive in a hand-tied cheesecloth covering. You'll need to make a permanent cover. Mary's original plans involved a quilt rack and a couple of women friends to help do the hand-tying. (I suggested she offer this as a three-day retreat at her house.)

My readers most likely don't have a quilt rack, so I offer this brilliant, easy alternative—a very simplified way to incorporate this wonderful wool batting onto the elegant beds of the 21st century.

1) Make a giant pillowcase out of two cotton (or flannel) sheets. Measure your wool batt, and allow 1" all around for seams. Sew three sides together, leaving the bottom open. Put 6" ties at the corners and on the sides.

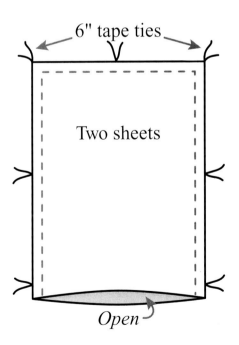

6" tape ties

Two sheets

Open

Step 1

2) Put the batting on top of the inside-out cover and sew loops to match the ties onto the inside corners of the wool batting. Tie the loops and ties to hold it securely, then turn.

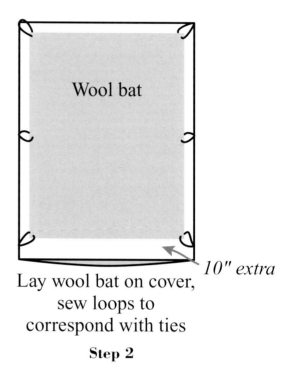

Lay wool bat on cover,
sew loops to
correspond with ties

Step 2

3) Use big safety pins around the edges, and at random places in the middle, to temporarily hold all the layers together.

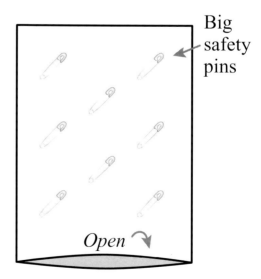

Turn: now the wool
bat is inside

Step 3

4) Roll the quilt up and sew the bottom shut with your sewing machine (you could also do this by hand, of course).

5) Hand-tie as shown. A tie every 10 inches should keep the batting in place.

This cover is now the permanent covering for your wool batt quilt.

To enjoy your new wool batting quilt, you simply insert it another decorative, duvet cover—the one your body will come into contact with and the one you'll take off the bed to wash.

Hand tie with yarn

Step 5

CORNER TIES

Whether goose down or wool batting, you'll want to keep your comforter in position inside the duvet cover. You could put grommets in the corners, like the Lands' End people. But ties and loops are easier. Pamela Burke recommends using twill tape to make your loops and ties. It's easy to sew, won't unravel, and will hold a knot. But, I was working on a project and didn't have any twill tape. In my usual hurry, I cut one-inch strips from an old worn out T-shirt and it worked great. The T-shirt fabric is easy to sew, won't unravel, and will hold a knot. It's also free. Here's the simple two-step process:

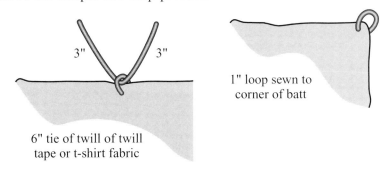

3"   3"

6" tie of twill of twill tape or t-shirt fabric

1" loop sewn to corner of batt

1) Turn your duvet cover inside out, and lay your comforter on top. Fold a 6" piece of twill tape (or whatever) in half, then, stitch the folded end securely into the four corners of the duvet cover. If desired, you can also place a tie in between the corners. Sew by hand, or pin it and machine stitch later.

2) On the duvet itself, use a 3" piece of twill tape, folded, and securely sew the open ends, making a *loop* to correspond with every place you've sewn a tie inside the duvet cover.

To assemble, turn the duvet cover inside out, lay the comforter on top, insert the ties into the loops, and tie knots. Then, turn the duvet cover right side out—and your comforter stays tight and secure inside.

Pam recommends adding a tie and loop every 20 inches along the inside top of a king-size duvet cover. If you only put them in the corners, you get a dip in the center of your duvet.

When it comes to making a decorative duvet cover, most of us are intimidated by the *closing* aspect of the thing: whether to do buttons, which would, of course, involve the dreaded buttonholes; or put in a zipper.

Most of us, if asked whether we'd like to sew, put in a 40" zipper, or nail Jell-O to a tree would pick the Jell-O project every time. Velcro is too stiff for a nice, elegant closure.

In Europe, they also do this on their pillowcases. Joanne Ross bought some gorgeous linen pillowcases when she went on a Husqvarna trip to Sweden.

Each pillowcase had two 6" long white twill tape ties hanging out the open end of the case. Two on each side. Duh! What an easy, classy, subtle way to keep your pillow in place.

In this picture, Amy and Cale are under a duvet cover made out of a vintage chenille bedspread. This is *so easy*. Just lay a sheet on the backside of your bedspread. Sew around three edges, leaving the bottom open. Use the corner-tie method to insert the comforter.

In this case, I left the bottom open, as I didn't want to interfere with the fringe of the bedspread. Of course, you could also sew on some additional twill tape ties.

Making new duvet covers is a *great* use for vintage bedspreads.

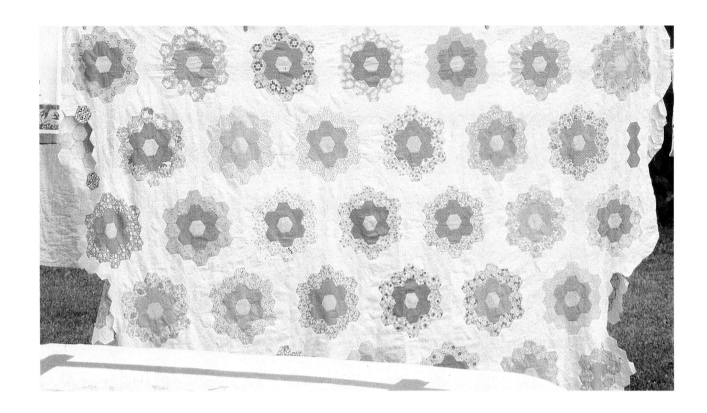

DUVET COVER FROM OLD QUILT TOPS

This wonderful Grandmother's Flower Garden quilt top, pictured above, was pieced by our great-grandmother. Unfortunately, it has been stored for forty years; my sister, Ronda, is the third generation to keep it in a closet. There is absolutely no chance that she will ever get this sucker completed. I told her it would make a great duvet cover—and she was delighted with the prospect of actually being able to use it on her bed.

I ran out of time, but I promised to get it done for her birthday next year. Every family has old quilt tops, right? This is a wonderful way to get them out of storage and on the beds, where they were meant to be. Make a duvet cover out of them.

BEDSPREADS

You don't need this book to figure out how to buy a new bedspread and/or quilt to fit your bed. Anybody can go shopping. There are wonderful things available on the market. Have a ball.

However, I would like to offer different ways to restyle an old double bedspread for your queen-size bed. Bring that vintage stuff your mother has in a trunk *back* onto the family beds.

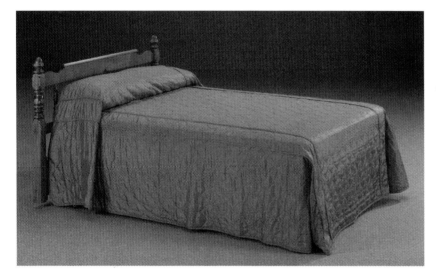

1. A purple satin bedspread on a double bed, as intended.

2. Here it is again, this time with a lace cover and an embroidered flat sham.

3. This time, you see the purple satin spread being used as a bed skirt on a queen-size bed. The lace bed cover is now serving as a second layer for the bed skirt.

4. Here is that same lace bed cover, being used alone as a bed skirt.

5. On this beautiful Bluebird bed, the quilt is only a twin size, but we've positioned it over a double-size white matellaise bedspread and used tablecloths for a layered bed skirt.

6. This is a double-size white bedspread on a queen-size bed. We boxed the corners. This is a great finishing detail and the ball fringe is just too charming.

Restyling an old double bedspread might save you some money, and it's considerably more creative than just going shopping, don't you think?

BLANKETS

Not everybody has gone down the "comforter" road. Some people still prefer blankets. My sister, Deena, likes the weight of a blanket. (Just wait until menopause, kiddo…) If you find a wonderful old blanket, but it's too small for your queen-size bed, don't be afraid to sew an extender on the end to tuck in at the bottom of your bed. It doesn't have to match, because nobody is really going to see it. I used to put a wool blanket on my bed, then a lightweight flannel blanket on top of it. I pull the light blanket further down, so that it is the only one tucked under the mattress—and it holds the heavier blanket in place.

WOOL

Wool is an excellent choice for a blanket. Pictured above is one of my favorite blankets *ever*. This beautiful "Orr Health" wool blanket, with the intricate woven tulip design, cost $12.50 at an auction.

Often, wool blankets have been stored with moth balls, and that smell can linger for a long time. Just bite the bullet and wash them in your home washing machine.

- Fill the tub with warm water and 1/2 cup of soap. Make sure the soap is dissolved.
- Add the blanket, and swish it around until it is completely wet.

- Let it sit for at least one hour.
- Run a regular washing cycle.
- Three cold water rinses (or, another washing cycle with no soap).
- DO NOT PUT YOUR WOOL BLANKET IN THE DRYER.
- In the old days, they used "stretchers" to make sure the blanket got back its original shape.
- I hang the blanket outside, cradled on a sheet, hung between two different clotheslines to help carry the weight of the wet wool. The sun also helps eliminate that moth ball odor.
- OR—lay the wet blanket on top of your bed, with rolled up towels to "lift" it, and place a fan directly on it to hurry up the drying process. It could take two days or so. *Never* put a wool blanket away damp.

When I was a kid, Saturday was always the day to change the beds in our four upstairs bedrooms. Mom would open up a window, lean out, and snap the blankets and bedspreads. She would shake them for a bit, then let them hang there, held by the window itself, until time to put it back on the bed. Every now and then, I drive by a house with bedding hanging out the windows and know exactly what they're doing.

Obviously, there are many kinds of blankets on the market today. I travel a lot and most hotels seem to favor those vellux blankets. It's like sleeping under polyester snot. You can certainly buy blankets made out of acrylic, polyester, and nylon. You just can't make me write about them.

Tip:

To store wool blankets, put them in a cedar chest or closet, inside a pillowcase, or wrapped in a cotton sheet. Never put them in a plastic bag. You don't have to wash them every year. Hanging them outside to "air out" is an old-fashioned and refreshing thing to do.

Chapter 10

Once Upon A Mattress

Most of my friends love to shop. Some even *live* to shop. But I never knew anybody who enjoyed spending money on a new mattress. It's like paying the light bill. You've got to do it, but who's gonna notice? Even men don't like mattress shopping (and they get a kick out of buying chipper/shredders). Give them this choice: new mattress, fishing gear, power tools, or new golf clubs. The mattress will be dead last every time—even if they don't fish or golf.

To begin my mattress education, I went to furniture stores to hear the sales "schpeal." For the record, I would rather have six root canals. In all fairness, these salespeople don't make any money until they *sell* something, and they're pretty good at it. It's *our* job to be informed consumers. It's a good idea to start on the phone and have a list of questions to ask.

Every year, the mattress companies try to convince us there have been big technological advances in their world—like they just reinvented the wheel. But, basically, a mattress is metal coils tied together, covered with something, topped with foam, then quilted.

Way More Than You Ever Wanted to Know

Most consumers fall for one or two myths during mattress-hunting season:

- Number of coils: Salespeople milk this for all it's worth. The truth is, you only have "x" amount of space in a mattress. Every time they add coils, the wire must get thinner. You could theoretically have so many coils each one would be as lightweight and thin as the weak little spring on an old-fashioned screen door.

- Mattress warranty: In this industry, the warranty is for "material defects." They could offer a 100-year warranty if they wanted to because, unless the bottom of your mattress falls out the day you plunk it down on your bed frame, anything and everything else falls under "normal wear and tear."

So, then, what questions *should* you be asking?

- Number of coils does matter. A decent queen-size mattress should contain 600-800 coils—and most of them do. Some companies put more coils in the middle third of the mattress, which seems like a good idea.

- Edge support: You want some kind of steel bracing around the outside edges of the mattress that will support the weight of sitting on the edge of the bed and then bounce back—again and again. The cheaper ones have Styrofoam sides (they use a much fancier word) that soon collapse. (But they call that normal wear and tear, remember?)

- 🕮 <u>Bed-top coil covering</u>: This is important. Instead of light-weight carpet padding, you want a fibrous pad, like sisal—something sturdy to create a lasting shield between the metal coils and the foam rubber.

- 🕮 <u>Foam padding</u>: Foam rubber is not all alike. A well-informed salesperson will show you how quickly the foam "recovers." Any thick foam will conform to your body, which initially feels soft and comfy, but cheap foam soon develops a permanent body indent—which is *not* comfortable.

- 🕮 <u>Fabric covering of mattress</u>: Beware the plastic-like polyester. If you perspire at night (and we all do), your body moisture gets trapped between your skin and the mattress, making for a soggy, clammy night of sleep. Instead, you want a sturdy quality fabric made of cotton/linen/wool, since natural fibers wick away your body moisture.

- 🕮 <u>Pillow-top filling</u>: Most pillow tops are filled with more foam rubber, or polyester fiberfill. The best pillow tops are filled with wool or even goose down. These natural materials wick away body moisture.

Lebeda is a Midwestern factory-direct mattress company founded in 1946. It manufactures mattresses in Marion, Iowa, with other stores in Illinois, Missouri, and Kansas. The local manager, Brian Herrick, spent quite a bit of time with me, answering many questions. Lebeda was also kind enough to provide the beds and mattresses for the pictures in this book.

After weeks of mattress shopping, I felt like the biggest difference was not necessarily in the quality of the mattress, but rather in the marketing, rents, and commissions being paid to the middle men. If you buy your mattress at a furniture store, they need to get an additional 30-percent mark-up, on top of the manufacturer. That's not true if you buy from a factory-direct mattress company like Lebeda. It manufactures the mattress and sells it out of its own stores.

In today's world of retail, you don't have the opportunity very often to buy a product directly from the guy who made it. I have no idea why it's still possible with mattresses, but I would encourage you to consider this as an option when you're in the market for a new bed. All the models who got to take naps on the Lededa beds were very impressed.

The danger of mattress shopping is that you may not get what you paid for. All the important stuff is covered with fabric, then upholstered. Only Superman, with his nifty X-ray vision, could tell for sure what he was getting. And, sadly, you won't know if you got high-quality foam or the cheesy worthless stuff until you've slept on it for about a year (ask me how I know this).

Good value and low price are seldom related.

Mattress Pads

Use a good quality, 100 percent cotton mattress pad on your mattress. Trust me—I'm right about this.

If you don't think you need one, call the local Kirby Vacuum people and ask them to vacuum your naked mattress. Be prepared to faint from disgust—90 percent of all household dust is caused by our skin "sloffing" off. That's what dust mites live on—our dead skin. Without a mattress pad, you're creating a perfect environment for them.

And if that dust mite village isn't enough to convince you, think about this: The average person loses two cups of water every night through "evaporation"—otherwise known as perspiration. It's normal. Healthy, even, but disgusting—especially when you think about your mattress absorbing all that sweat, day after day, week after week, month after month, year after year. Combine that with the dead skin.

A good mattress pad will absorb most of that, wick it away, and save your mattress. Cotton mattress pads are available at all the better department stores, and linen chain stores. You should be able to find a queen size for under $50. Your sheets will also fit better. You don't have to wash the mattress pad every week. Every couple of months is fine.

Featherbeds

The ultimate mattress pad is an actual featherbed that goes on top of your mattress.

Many years ago, a featherbed would be placed on top of rope lacings, or into woven flat metal frames. A featherbed *was* the mattress. But, just like horse-drawn carriages were pushed off the road by gas-powered automobiles, featherbeds became obsolete once steel coil mattresses were widely available.

But now they're back, although today we use them in a very different way. Instead of being the mattress, they have become a luxurious accessory for the top of the mattress. I knew a trend must be developing when I started to see them on the home-shopping channels.

You might consider wool batting for an "underquilt." My friend Valerie has arthritis and fibromyalgia and she is a big fan of sleeping on wool. The proper way to make a bed when using a wool underquilt is to put a deep-pocket fitted sheet right on top of the wool as a kind of liner. Then, use your usual fitted sheet over that. This makes sense to me, and is probably the way you would make the bed if you were using a featherbed as well.

Care and Maintenance of Mattresses

Normal recommended "care" for a mattress used to be to turn it over every year. With the new pillow tops, that's no longer possible. But you still should shift it from end to end twice a year. Vacuum your mattress and pillows every time you change your sheets. I wasn't taught to do that (maybe I just wasn't paying attention). A good vacuum is a wonderful tool for keeping your mattress and/or pillows clean.

Hey—I know it isn't exciting to think about buying a new mattress. But it's important. There is no point in putting luxurious linens on a poor-quality, uncomfortable mattress. That would be like putting delicious fresh cream cheese frosting on a hard, crumbly, stale old chocolate cake. You aren't going to fool anybody.

My Grandma used to say, "You can't make a silk purse out of a sow's ear." Gee, I love to use old farmer clichés to make a point.

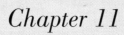

Chapter 11

Pillow Talk

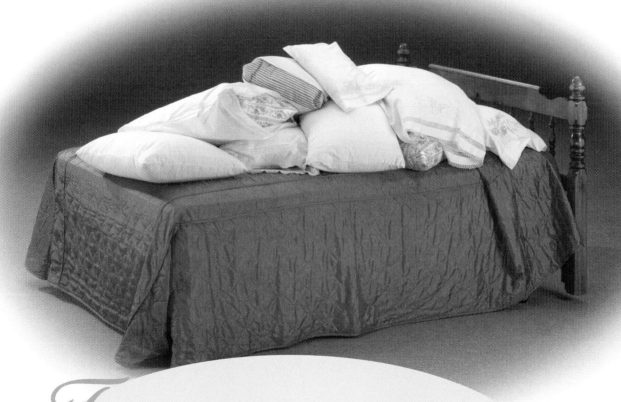

The pillow is the most personal item on your bed. *To each his own* really is the principle that applies here. Every married couple I know experienced *the* pillow transition. They started off with two identical pillows. But, at some point, *hers* became hers and *his* became his—and nobody can pinpoint the exact moment it happened. Maybe pillows are like a good marriage. Being happy isn't always about wanting the same things. It's about learning to accept another person's personal likes and dislikes—then respecting each other's differences.

Does Size Matter?

Like beds, pillows come in all sizes. In my opinion, with pillows, it's mostly a merchandising technique. The bigger queen-size bed had real benefits for us—like more room for two people to roll over at night. But there should be just *one* head rolling on each pillow, right? If you like to bunch your pillow up, or punch it down, a bigger pillow might even work against you. Thank God nobody I know has a head big enough to warrant a king-size pillow. Well, with the possible exception of some 18-year-old boys.

Mary Mulari disagrees with me, and she thinks standard-size pillows look too small on her queen-size bed.

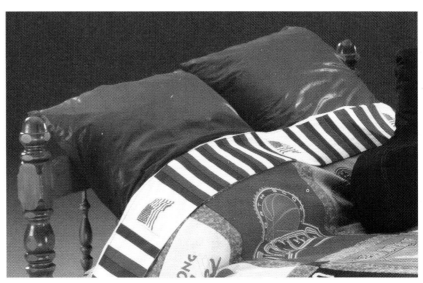

The newest size in Pillow World is the "European square," but it's too soon to know whether it's a lasting trend or just a fad. I have no idea where this came from, although I suspect Martha Stewart had something to do with it.

The big square pillows shown in the photo above look great on a bed. Ah, but I have some wonderful old vintage pillow shams that were made for big "square" pillows. So maybe they're not new at all. Just goes to show you that sooner or later, everything that goes around comes around again. But most people consider these big square pillows purely decorative: fine to dress up the bed, but put aside at night. If you want back support as you read or watch television in bed, you'll positively need a backrest pillow, shown at left. I thought about including a pattern so you could sew your own, but then I remembered they cost less than $20 and you have a life.

It's What's on the Inside That Counts

GOOSE DOWN

Top choice for pillows on an elegant bed would be white goose down.

Of course, everything I wrote about feathers and down in Chapter 9 applies here. New white goose down pillows are expensive. Maybe $100 each. Be sure to feel the pillow with your fingers, looking for feather quills. Real down doesn't have those little pokies. The ticking must be of a very high thread count to prevent the down from popping out during use. Down pillows may seem expensive, but remember—you will have this pillow for the rest of your life. Down will last much longer than any of us will.

With Ritaluck, I often find old down/feather pillows at auctions. I used to take them to the local dry cleaners and have them cleaned, sanitized, and reticked for about $8 each. Over the years, I've gotten a dozen beautiful pillows in this way, and I often give them as gifts. Last year, I gave one to my Aunt Glad, who is 90 years and lives in a nursing home. Two weeks later, she called me and said there was something wrong with her pillow. Sure enough, her beautiful new down pillow had morphed into a flat, stained old foam rubber piece of crud. Probably an honest mistake on the part of the people who make the beds. They have a lot of things to keep straight. On the next down pillow I gave her, I wrote "AUNT GLAD" right on the ticking (in permanent black laundry marker). Then, as a helpful reminder, I wrote her name and room number in smaller print.

You can wash your down/feather pillows yourself. The directions are in Chapter 9 (follow the same procedure as for the goose-down comforter). But, don't think this is an easy job. It takes all day and you will feel like you're baby-sitting a two-year-old. The first time I did it, I was terrified that the pillows would bust open and I'd have feathers everywhere, so I kept checking on them every 15 minutes. Keeping the pillows under the water was the hardest part, even after I weighed them down with jugs full of water. My two pillows kept wanting to bounce up and float on top and I worried they weren't getting any soap or water inside the pillow ticking.

In the end, though, this is worth the effort. My pillows smell wonderful and fresh, and that heavy cotton striped ticking got softer and very bright looking. Doing this job turned out to be very satisfying. From now on, I'm going to wash my pillows once a year. Well, maybe just on the odd years.

NOT WHITE GOOSE DOWN
Polyester Fiberfill

The truth is, most of the pillows on the retail market are filled with polyester fiberfill. Most of these pillows cost $10 or so. Some really top-of-the-line models have a foam core that is surrounded by fiberfill. They might run you $20 apiece. Manufacturers usually recommend that these pillows be washed and not dry-cleaned. If they get lumpy, or the filling shifts too much, just buy new ones.

Foam Rubber

You can also buy pillows filled only with foam rubber. They used to shred it (those were really bad smelly pillows). Nowadays, they form it into an ergonomic shape. Enough said about foam-rubber pillows.

Buckwheat Hulls

The new-kid-on-the-block in Pillow World is the buckwheat-hull pillow. Here in Iowa, we didn't know about buckwheat-hull pillows until they started running the infomercial on late-night television last year.

Buckwheat-hull pillows are usually small, maybe half the size of a standard pillow. They cost about $20 each, conform to your head, provide excellent support, and wick away moisture and heat.

Wool Batting

This is a brand new development in Pillow World. They are making bed pillows out of 100 percent natural wool. Because of the uncanny property of wool to absorb 30 percent of its weight in moisture, (remember those sheep?) a wool pillow seems like a wonderful alternative. At this time, they are available only in the standard size and cost about $30 per pillow. If you have an allergy to feathers, wool may be the answer.

Pillow Protectors

Like mattress pads, these pillowcase-like protectors with a zipper at one end are an integral part of a comfortable, luxurious bed. They are readily available at any department store and you should *always* have them on your pillows. I wash them every couple of months, or when they need it. They cost maybe $6 each and are worth every penny.

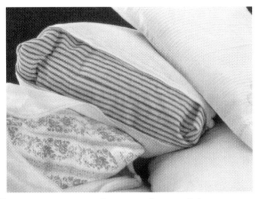

When shopping for pillow protectors, the usual two things apply: 100 percent cotton fabric (breathing and wicking), with a high thread count of 200 and up.

You might want to make your own pillow protector, especially if your pillow is an unusual size. If you don't have the time to make one and can't find one to purchase, you could use an old pillowcase as a liner, then put on your decorative pillowcase.

If you don't use pillow protectors, I have just one word for you: drool.

Consider giving a pillow as a gift to somebody you love. Not just any pillow, of course. A white goose down pillow that will last a lifetime. My Mom gave down/feather pillows to my sons Ross and Elliott. She reticked feathers that had originally come from her mother-in-law, Pearl Little. At the time, my boys were very young and didn't appreciate the pillow gift. They would have preferred a remote-control car or maybe a plastic action figure.

But, Elliott is 20 now, and he sleeps on his pillow every night. Ross, 24, took his with him when he went away to college, and into every apartment since.

I like the idea that wherever they go, the pillows they sleep on every night provide a loving connection to this family.

If pillows really could talk, my boys would hear their Grandma's voice whispering, "Sweet dreams…"

Chapter 12

The Art of Bedmaking

"Pequot sheets and pillowcases are as perfect as human ingenuity, skill, and care can make them.
Pequot Sheeting on a badly made bed gives no pleasure, and sets our own efforts at naught."
—1929 *Story of Pequot*

Beds are like people: each unique and individual. Making the perfect bed isn't like algebra with only one right answer, but more like painting a beautiful work of art and then putting yourself in the picture. The point of this book is to make your bed an inviting place where you feel relaxed and tranquil. Sanctuary—that soft place to fall into. You can create that restful, loving feeling with elegant linen, luxurious comforters, and fresh scents.

Hopefully, now you will recognize quality and then seek it out when shopping for your bed. By now, you know the mantras: Express yourself. Don't be afraid. Enjoy it. Make it something special. Embellish it. Personalize it. Have fun with it. Change it with the seasons. Revel in the luxury. Make it incredible. Spoil your family. They deserve it. Spoil yourself. You deserve it.

Whenever I bought a vintage crocheted sheet or a set of embroidered pillowcases, I felt connected to the women who came before me. To our grandmothers and great-grandmothers—those female ancestors who spent countless hours tatting wide lace borders onto the family bedding. There was so much love in their needlework; in every bed they made.

I wrote this book so they and their beautiful, loving work would not be forgotten; so it could be passed along to the next generation of women. The children born to the baby boomers—our daughters, my nieces. These young women will become the keepers of the family beds. They will inherit the heirlooms, preserve the family traditions. Hopefully, they'll start some new ones of their own.

This last chapter on "Bedmaking" is especially dedicated to my young newlywed friend, Carrie Fitzgerald. (Oops—Carrie Parrott now!) I saw Carrie nearly every day of her childhood. She is my cousin, Kim's, daughter, and she was only 12 years old when she started to get off the school bus on Tuesdays to help me clean and make my family beds. Carrie taught me to be a better housekeeper, and I taught her about vintage linens. Her interest and enthusiasm gave me the encouragement I needed to write this book. For a wedding gift, I gave Carrie and Steve the lavender Ralph Lauren Polo sheet set that I made out of two flat sheets. Whenever Carrie would go shopping for Steve, she'd say, "It's time for a trip to POLOland." I always knew they would get the lavender POLO sheets as a wedding gift. The fact that the antique lavender and green quilt matches the sheets so perfectly is just more Ritaluck.

Sue Evans is my best friend from high school. Her daughter, Kara, was getting married at the time I was working on this book. I was delighted when Kara and her fiancé, Scott, bought the Lebeda bed featured on the cover of this book. On the front of the wedding card I made for them, I scanned in a picture of the book cover.

On the inside of the card, I wrote:

Here's what I know to be true:

*You'll spend a third of your life in bed— take some care to
make it a comfortable, soft place to fall into.*

*Cotton is better than polyester. One is real— the other is a pre-
tender. People are just like fabric—learn the difference.
Then always go with cotton.*

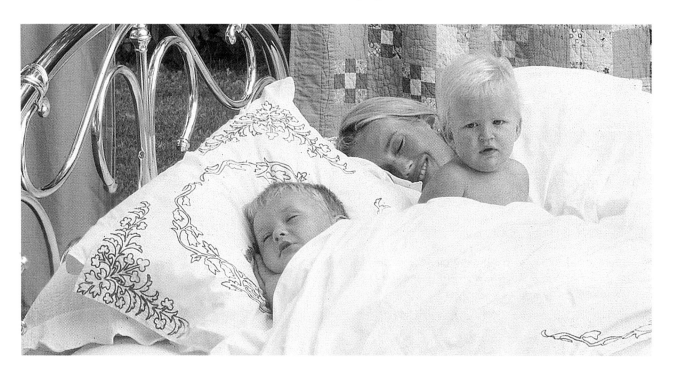

Here's the most important thing: Give yourself permission to
always use your best stuff. Enjoy it. Don't hold anything back for
a special occasion. Every time I serve cheesecake, I use Aunt
Rozella's Spring Glory forks.

*Because life **is** the special occasion.*

Glossary

Chenille: A fuzzy cotton yarn or fabric that has pile protruding around it. Chenille is the French word for "caterpillar."

Damask: A cotton fabric made on a jacquard loom, creating a pattern. Most often seen in tablecloths and napkins.

Down: The very soft, shaftless, fluffy clusters which come from the breast and underbelly of ducks and geese.

Duvet: Duvet means comforter, and comforter means duvet. Picture a big, bed-sized pillowcase filled with something (polyester, feathers, or wool batt).

Egyptian cotton: Although Egyptian cotton is a variety of long staple cotton, buyer beware. Manufacturers are not required to divulge the percentage of actual "Egyptian" cotton contained in their finished goods.

Extra long staple cotton: This means that the cotton fiber is at least 1-1/16 inches long. The three varieties of ELS cotton are: Egyptian, Sea Island, and Pima.

Flannel: A plain weave cotton cloth that is heavily brushed to create a soft finish.

Hospital corner: When making a bed, the technique of folding and tucking the bottom corners of the top sheet between the mattress and the box spring, to keep the sheet from coming undone during sleep.

Loft: When something is full of air, or puffy-enough so that when pressed, it will spring back to its original size, i.e., down, feathers, wool batt.

Matelasse: A heavy jacquard-woven cotton fabric, often used for bedspreads. The pattern stands out to give a three-dimensional, almost quilted look.

Muslin: A woven cotton sheeting with a thread count of 140 or less per square inch.

Percale: A smooth, finely combed woven sheeting with a minimum thread count of 180 threads per square inch.

Quilt: Typically, a patchwork of different colored fabrics put together in an elaborate pattern for the top. For assembly, a plain back would be sewn on, and a layer of cotton or wool batting would be in the middle.

Ritaluck: The parking lot at Kohl's is jam-packed, but on your first pass, a car in the first parking space is backing out. If this happens to you 20 times in a row, you've got Ritaluck.

Sateen: A satin weave fabric with a smooth shiny surface. Instead of simple over and under weaving, a sateen would typically go over two, and under one.

Sheeting: Plain woven, carded cotton yarn cloth in medium and heavy weights. When the thread count is low, sheeting is defined as muslin. When the thread count is high, and the yarn is combed, sheeting is defined as percale.

SUPIMA™: A registered trademark of the American Pima Grower's Association. This always means that the cotton you are buying is 100 percent extra-long Staple PIMA cotton. In my humble opinion, this is the best cotton on the market.

Thread count: The number of threads in a square inch of finished fabric. The finer the threads, the higher the thread count.

Wicking: The term used to describe that property whereby moisture is absorbed, then evaporated, away from your body.

Wool batt: Wool from sheep that's simply scoured and carded; then, it's combed to a certain size, and sandwiched between layers of cheesecloth so it will retain its shape.

Resources

The best place for you to look for vintage linen inspirations in your own life may be that cedar-lined hope chest you inherited from your Grandma. If you don't have any luck there, be on the lookout at Goodwill stores, antiques stores, estate sales, and auctions. And don't forget the Internet. There is some great stuff on the auction site eBay (www.ebay.com) I probably shouldn't be telling you this, but the site actually has a category called "Antique Linens."

To get in touch with me, see where I may be speaking, or find out about buying wool batt:
Rita Farro
P.O. Box 421
Princeton, IA 52768
Email: ritafar@aol.com
www.dressyourdreambed.com

For a fine selection of sewing notions and supplies:
Nancy's Notions
(800) 833-0690
www.nancysnotions.com

To see where Mary Mulari is speaking, or find out about her latest books:
Mary Mulari
Box 87
Aurora, MN 55705
www.marymulari.com

For more information and education about cotton:
Cotton incorporated
www.cottoninc.com

To find out about the best sewing machines and sergers in the world:
(800) 358-0001
www.husqvarnaviking.com

Okay-here's my biggest treasure hunting tip: Buy irregular sets of Charisma sheets, SUPIMA cotton, 310 TC. Trust me. This information is worth the whole price of this book. For more information, contact:
www.fieldcrestcannonoutlet.com
(800) 841-3336